THE COMING
SPIRITUAL
EARTHQUAKE

JAMES T. HARMAN

PROPHECY COUNTDOWN PUBLICATIONS

THE COMING SPIRITUAL EARTHQUAKE

ISBN 0-9636984-0-0

Library of Congress Catalog Card Number 93-92712

Scripture quotations are from the Thompson Chain Reference Bible, New International Version. Copyright 1973, 1978, and 1984 by the International Bible Society.

Scripture quotations identified LB are from The Living Bible, Copyright 1971 by Tyndale House Publishers, Inc., Wheaton, IL. All rights reserved.

Scripture quotations identified KJ are the King James Version.

Numbered references to selected words are from James H. Strong's Dictionaries of the Hebrew and Greek Words.

Cover design by Tim Kittell.

PROPHECY COUNTDOWN PUBLICATIONS
P.O. Box 941612
Maitland, FL 32794

Prologue

The message of this book was born from a horrifying dream I had in which I found myself in the period the Bible describes as the Tribulation.

I seldom dream; however, this dream was so real and terrifying that it motivated me to search the Scriptures to determine who will be able to escape this dreadful time of testing, and how a person can prepare.

I believe the Lord gave me this in order to help people prepare to be "found worthy to escape" the Tribulation. It is my prayer it will be used by our loving, heavenly Father to touch the lives of those He wants to reach with this <u>urgent</u> message.

In His Love,
Jim Harman

Dedication

This book is dedicated to all Overcoming, First Fruit believers, looking for the soon return of our loving Lord and Savior, Jesus Christ.

Table of Contents

Foreword

I'm convinced no message is more exciting than the message of our Lord's Return for His Own. It is the "Blessed Hope" of the believer in Christ. It is the message of this book.

However, when prophecy scholars lose sight of this message and get caught up in, and devote more time to the New Age Movement or the New World Order, than to our Lord's Coming, there should be great concern.

And, there is great concern for those who believe their profession of faith in Christ is all that is needed to prepare one for the Rapture when the Lord comes for His Own. While coming to know Christ as Saviour is absolutely important, there are many admonitions given to believers to "watch" and "be ready" for our Lord's Coming.

Surely revival must come to the heart of the person living in known disobedience to the will of God upon realizing their carelessness and indifference. This condition, which constitutes "lukewarmness," could result in their lack of being ready when our Lord returns.

If looking for our Lord's Return, will we not want to be ready for that glorious event? As we read in I John 3:2-3, *". . . when He shall appear, we shall be like Him; for we shall see Him as He is. And every man that hath this hope in Him, purifieth himself, even as He is pure."*

The message presented in **THE COMING SPIRITUAL EARTHQUAKE** is greatly needed to awaken believers to the false assumptions many have when it comes to the Rapture. This book will be used by the Holy Spirit to awaken you to the nearness of our Lord's Return, along with preparing you: to the need of living daily for Christ; to be ready when He comes. May God grant it. Amen.

Ray Brubaker
God's News Behind the News

Preface

One of the biggest false ideas in the church today is that all Christians will be going in the Rapture when Jesus Christ snatches His Bride up to the throne.

One of the second biggest false ideas is that no one knows when it is going to be. By not properly interpreting the Word of God, these misconceptions have greatly contributed to the lukewarm condition of the church today. Jesus Christ foresaw this current state and warned the present church in Revelation 3:16:

> "So then because thou art lukewarm, and neither cold nor hot, I will spew thee out of my mouth."

There is coming a great SPIRITUAL EARTHQUAKE that will shake the Church. Many will wake up to find they are part of the multitude of believers living in the Tribulation period.

This book is a final warning to the Church:

REPENT, THE KINGDOM OF
HEAVEN IS AT HAND.

May God use this message to awaken many in our churches in order to prepare to meet the Bridegroom.

It is time for the WISE VIRGINS to trim their lamps and ***be ready*** to enter into the marriage chamber (Matthew 25).

Only those who have ***KEPT*** His Word and who are found ***LOOKING*** for Him will be counted worthy to escape the coming tribulation. All others will be tried in the time of testing to be ushered in by the COMING SPIRITUAL EARTHQUAKE.

Introduction

Debate has gone on for years as to whether Jesus would return before the Tribulation period (pre-trib), in the middle of it (mid-trib) or at its end (post-trib).

This confusion has fostered an attitude that prophecy is too difficult to understand for the average Christian. As a result, the REAL truth in the Word of God has remained hidden from the believer.

CRITICAL TIME

The CHURCH is at a **VERY CRITICAL POINT**. Jesus is getting ready to remove His First Fruit Believers from this planet, to be followed by the horrible Tribulation period.

Revelation 7:9-17, warns of a GREAT MULTITUDE which no man could number, coming out of the great Tribulation period. It will be shown that these represent many in our churches today for whom martyrdom will be required as described in Revelation 12:11.

TIME TO PREPARE

Prior to the Rapture, all Christians are given the opportunity of preparing for that event. Those who are Overcomers, counted worthy to escape the tribulation period, will be caught up to the throne of God, while all others will be required to be Overcomers by not shrinking from death.

It is time for the Church to **WAKE UP** and **REPENT** before it is too late. The COMING SPIRITUAL EARTHQUAKE will be far more devastating than any economic earthquake or shaking of the earth's surface!

TIMING OF EVENTS

In an attempt to determine when the Lord is going to return, many dates have been set and many have been disappointed when those dates have come and gone.

Because of this, popular tradition has emerged that it is wrong to set dates and that we are not supposed to know when the Lord is going to return.

This presents a problem since we are rapidly approaching the *COMING SPIRITUAL EARTHQUAKE*, and many believers will be taken by surprise. The day is almost upon us, and Paul warned us in I Thessalonians 5:4:

> "But you, brothers, are not in darkness so that this day **SHOULD** surprise you like a thief."

Paul is telling us that Christians SHOULD NOT be surprised. By implication, Paul was saying that some Christians will indeed be surprised, even though they should not be taken by surprise.

Hosea 4:6 warns us:

"My people are destroyed for lack of knowledge: because thou hast rejected knowledge, I will also reject thee. . . . "

Christians need to return to the Holy Word of God to see what it says about knowing when the Lord is going to return. Instead of listening to church tradition, this book will help the believer better understand what God's Word has to say about the timing of end-time events that are about to culminate in the COMING SPIRITUAL EARTHQUAKE.

Readers need to approach this material with an open mind, teachable spirit and heart of love. We all need to be like the Berean Christians who searched the Scriptures daily to be sure what even the Apostle Paul told them was the truth (see Acts 17:11).

If believers fail to properly divide the Word of Truth (II Timothy 2:15), they will be misguided and may find themselves in the horror of the Tribulation period. Jesus warned us of this in Matthew 23:13-14:

"Woe to you, teachers of the law and Pharisees, you hypocrites! You shut the kingdom of heaven in men's faces. You yourselves do not enter, nor will you let those enter who are trying to."

Jesus was admonishing the Church leaders! The very ones that should know the Truth are actually keeping others from finding the correct way!

One of the main purposes of this book is to help guide people back to what the Word of God actually says and to help them **prepare** to meet the Bridegroom.

CHAPTER 1

Wise Will Understand

As the Church approaches the end of the sixth millennium it would be wise to listen to the words of Apostle Paul's companion and fellow-preacher Barnabas:

"And even in the beginning of the creation he makes mention of the sabbath. And God made in the SIX DAYS the works of his hands; and he finished them on the seventh day, and rested the seventh day, and sanctified it.

"Consider, my children, what that signifies, he finished them in six days. The meaning of it is this; that in SIX THOUSAND YEARS the Lord God will bring all things to AN END.

"For with him ONE DAY is a THOUSAND YEARS; as himself testifieth, saying, Behold this day shall be as a thousand years. Therefore, children, in SIX DAYS, that is, in SIX THOUSAND YEARS shall all things be accomplished" (Barnabas 13:3-5).

This sounds strikingly similar to what the Apostle Peter had to say when discussing the end times:

"But ***DO NOT FORGET*** this one thing, dear

friends: WITH THE LORD A DAY IS LIKE A THOU-
SAND YEARS, and A THOUSAND YEARS ARE
LIKE A DAY . . . " (II Peter 3:8).

Both Barnabas and Peter were telling us how God measures
time. A day in His time frame is the equivalent to 1,000 years in
the life of man. Since He created the earth in 6 days and then
rested on the seventh, He was giving mankind a prophecy of how
long He was going to deal with the human race on this earth.

At the end of 6 days or 6,000 years, His Word will be finished
and mankind will then move into the 1,000 years of rest described in the book of Revelation.

There were approximately 4,000 years from creation until
Christ, giving us 2,000 years since His birth to arrive at a total of
6,000 years. In later chapters we will discuss exactly where we
are in this 2,000 year time frame.

SCIENCE CONFIRMS GOD'S WORD

The theory of relativity states that as you approach the speed
of light, time slows down. Let's assume that Jesus is able to
travel at the speed of light. Traveling at that speed for just 2 days,
by His clock, would represent nearly 2,000 years on the earth. In
other words, since Jesus left this earth about 2,000 years ago,
He has only been gone about 2 days in His time frame.

With this understanding, the words by the prophet Hosea
bring on added importance:

"After TWO DAYS he will revive us; on the THIRD
DAY he will restore us, that we may live in his presence"
(Hosea 6:2).

This is a prophecy that after two days, or 2,000 years in our
time frame, God will restore us to live in His presence. After the
second day we will dwell with the Lord in the coming Millen-

nium (His third day).

This time relationship is also spoken of by our Lord in several instances. One example is found in John 2:1: "On the THIRD DAY a wedding took place. . . . " This was a prophecy that after the end of the second day, or on the third day the Wedding described in Revelation 19:7, will take place. Two thousand years after the first coming of Christ, the Bride will rejoice at her Wedding to the Lamb at the start of the 1,000 year millennium reign.

The Word of God is a rich and wonderful store-house for those who are diligently seeking His truth. God has a master plan for mankind that is rapidly winding to a close.

RELIGIOUS SPIRIT

Whenever a date for the Lord's return is set, the first objection that most people make is, "You can't know the DAY or the HOUR, therefore let's not even discuss it." The argument goes on to say that it is wrong to set dates and that no one knows when Jesus is going to return.

Let's be careful that we are not like the Pharisees and Sadducees who were rebuked by Jesus himself in Matthew 16:2-3, KJ:

"When it is evening ye say, 'It will be fair weather; for the sky is red.' And in the morning, 'It will be foul weather today: for the sky is red and lowring.' O YE HYPOCRITES, ye can discern the face of the sky; but can ye not discern the SIGNS OF THE TIMES?"

The religious leaders at the time of Christ were rebuked because they could not discern the time that they were living in. As we will see in a subsequent chapter, had they read the Scripture with a proper heart, they would have known the TIME they were living in and they would have known to be LOOKING for their Messiah. In a similar manner, we are currently living at a time when the Scriptures are **SHOUTING:** *JESUS IS COM-ING!* Unfortunately, not everyone has the "ears to hear" or the "eyes to see" what is transpiring before them.

Because of the tradition that we cannot know about the timing of end-time events, many people will be caught off guard at the COMING SPIRITUAL EARTHQUAKE.

DAY AND HOUR

To ensure that we are not rebuked by Jesus, let's take a better look at what the Word of God has to say about knowing the timing.

The most widely used verse people quote when they want to prove that we are not to know when Jesus is returning is found in Matthew:

> "But of that day and hour knoweth no man, no, not the angels of heaven, but my Father only" (Matthew 24:36, KJ).

What most people fail to remember, however, is the preceding verse:

> "Heaven and earth shall PASS AWAY, but my words shall not pass away" (Matthew 24:35).

The day and hour that no one knew about when Jesus spoke those words was when heaven and earth will pass away at the end of the 1,000 year Millennium. The timing of when this will occur is found in Revelation 21:1:

> "Then I saw a new heaven and a new earth, for the first heaven and the first earth HAD PASSED AWAY."

The reason that this time is not known is found in Revelation

20:3, which says Satan is let out of the bottomless pit at the end of 1,000 years for: "a LITTLE SEASON." No one but God knows how long Satan will have to deceive the nations at that time.

HOUR YOU THINK NOT

The next objection to knowing the timing of end-time events is related to the following verses in Matthew 24:42-44, KJ:

> "WATCH therefore: for YE KNOW NOT WHAT HOUR your Lord doth come. But know this, that if the GOODMAN of the house had known in what WATCH the THIEF would come, he would not have suffered his house to be broken up. Therefore be ye also ready: for in such AN HOUR AS YE THINK NOT the Son of man cometh."

On the surface of things, it appears that the Lord is coming as a THIEF and at a time we will not know. For the answer to this, we need to turn over to the parallel passage in Luke where Peter asks the Lord a very vital question in Luke 12:39-41, KJ:

> "And this know, that if the goodman of the house had known what hour the thief would come, he would have watched, and not suffered his house to be broken through. Be ye therefore ready also: for the Son of Man cometh at AN HOUR WHEN YE THINK NOT.
>
> "Then Peter said unto him, LORD, SPEAKEST THOU THIS PARABLE UNTO US, OR EVEN TO ALL?"

In this parallel passage concerning when the Lord is going to return, Luke records a very important question that Peter asks: Is this parable for US, meaning fellow believers, or for everyone?

Before we look at the Lord's answer, let's remember why the

Lord spoke in parables:

> ". . . Why do you speak to them in parables? He
> replied, 'The knowledge of the secrets of the kingdom
> of heaven has been given to you, but not to them' "
> (Matthew 13:10&11).

> "Unto you it is given to know the mystery of the
> kingdom of God: but unto them that are without, all these
> things are done in parables: That seeing they may see,
> and not perceive; and hearing they may hear, and not
> understand" (Mark 4:11&12).

Jesus used parables, because not everyone is given knowledge to the mysteries of the kingdom. Peter's question about who Jesus meant in the parable of not knowing the timing becomes an essential point.

Now, let's see what the Lord's answer is to this crucial question:

> "And the Lord said, Who then is that FAITHFUL
> and WISE steward, whom HIS lord shall make ruler over
> his household, to give them their portion of meat in due
> season.

> "Blessed is THAT servant, whom his lord when he
> cometh shall find so doing. Of a truth I say unto you, that
> he will make him ruler over all that he hath.

> "But and if that servant say in his HEART, My lord
> delayeth his coming; and shall begin to beat the menser-
> vants and maidens, and to eat and drink, and to be
> drunken; The lord of that servant will COME IN A DAY
> WHEN HE LOOKETH NOT for him, and at AN HOUR
> WHEN HE IS NOT AWARE, and will cut him in
> sunder, and will appoint him his portion with the unbe-
> lievers" (Luke 12:42-46, KJ).

First of all, Jesus says that the FAITHFUL and WISE steward will be greatly blessed. They are dressed and READY with their lamps burning brightly WAITING and WATCHING for their Lord to return (see Luke 12:35&36 and Matthew 25:10).

But notice what the UNFAITHFUL servant is thinking in his heart: "My lord delayeth his coming." He is not LOOKING and WATCHING as the faithful and wise steward is. Instead, he is beating (Greek: wounding the conscience of) his brothers and sisters. He is saying: NO ONE KNOWS when the Lord is coming, so let's forget about it and talk about something else; let's concern ourselves with this present time and enjoy ourselves.

Because of the attitude of the unfaithful servant's heart, Jesus says that He comes for him: "in a DAY when he LOOKETH NOT FOR HIM, and at an HOUR WHEN HE IS NOT AWARE." To the unfaithful servant Jesus is coming like a thief. He is going to take him by surprise on a DAY AND HOUR that he will not expect Him.

The wise and faithful servant will be ready, waiting and watching for Jesus, while the unfaithful servant will not know and will be taken by surprise.

THIEF IN THE NIGHT

This teaching that the wise and faithful will know and the unfaithful will not know is also confirmed for us by Paul:

"Now, BROTHERS, about times and dates we do not need to write to you, for you know very well that the day of the Lord will come LIKE A THIEF in the night. While people are saying, 'Peace and safety,' destruction will come on THEM SUDDENLY, as labor pains on a pregnant woman, and they will not escape" (I Thessalonians 5:1-3).

Most people stop reading at the end of the third verse to try to prove their point that the Lord is going to come as a THIEF. He is coming like a THIEF, but to whom is He coming to as a THIEF? Notice what Paul says in the fourth verse:

> "But you, BROTHERS, are not in darkness so that this DAY SHOULD SURPRISE you like a THIEF."

Paul is saying that the Lord's coming should not surprise the Christian (BROTHER). While the rest of the world will be surprised like a THIEF, the true Christian **SHOULD NOT** be surprised.

This confirms what Jesus was teaching us in His parables. The wise and faithful steward will be READY, WAITING and WATCHING for Him when He comes for him. The unfaithful and foolish servant will not be looking for Him and will be taken by surprise.

LOOKING FOR JESUS

Further evidence for this teaching is found in the book of Hebrews. Hebrews 10:25 shows that the faithful servant will, "SEE THE DAY APPROACHING." How could we see the day coming if we are not supposed to know? By simple implication, we should know.

Not only should we know, but more importantly we should be LOOKING for Him as taught to us in Hebrews 9:28:

> "So Christ was once offered to bear the sins of many; and **UNTO THEM** that *LOOK FOR HIM* shall he appear the second time without sin unto salvation."

This makes it quite clear, Jesus is returning the second time for those who are LOOKING FOR HIM. In subsequent chapters we will review what looking for Him entails, and the fate of those who fail to heed God's Word.

Further, the book of Revelation implies the faithful will know when the Lord is coming:

"I know your deeds; you have a reputation of being alive, but you are dead. WAKE UP! Strengthen what remains and is about to die. . . . Remember, therefore, what you have received and heard; obey it, and repent. BUT IF YOU DO NOT WAKE UP, I will come LIKE A THIEF, and you will NOT KNOW at WHAT TIME I will come to you" (Revelation 3:2-3).

The church of Sardis was dead. The Lord rebuked it and warned it to repent and to wake up. By implication, if this church will only obey His admonition, they will not be surprised like a thief and they will **KNOW** the **TIME.**

The Word of God is very clear. The wise and faithful servant will be looking for Jesus and they will be ready, waiting and watching for Him. They will know the time and will not be taken by surprise.

The unfaithful and foolish servant will not know when Jesus returns and they will not be ready for Him. They will be taken by surprise like a thief and they will not know the day or hour when He will return.

The choice is left up to the individual. He can heed the Word of God and be looking for the soon return of Jesus, or else he can continue listening to the tradition of not knowing and be taken by surprise like a thief.

KNOW IT IS NEAR

Finally, Jesus commanded us to *KNOW* the timing of end-time events:

"Now learn a parable of the fig tree; When his branch is yet tender, and putteth forth leaves, ye know that summer is nigh:

"So likewise ye, when ye shall see all these things, **KNOW** THAT IT IS NEAR, EVEN AT THE DOORS" (Matthew 24:32-33, KJ).

Just prior to telling us the fig tree parable, Jesus listed all of the signs that we would see, such as: wars and rumors of wars, nation rising against nation, famines and earthquakes in diverse places. These signs were just the beginning of birth pains, indicating that the time for delivery (Tribulation period) was just about due.

Then Jesus gives us one of the most important clues to knowing His return is near. He tells us to LEARN a parable or lesson about the FIG TREE. Most bible students agree that the Fig Tree represents the nation of Israel (see Hosea 9:10 and Joel 1:6-7).

Until this century, Israel had been scattered throughout the world with no land to call home. Then on May 14, 1948, the state of Israel was founded and on May 15, 1949, was recognized by the United Nations.

Jesus tells us that once we see the nation of Israel established again we can and SHOULD KNOW that His return is near, even at the DOOR!

When someone knocks on your door or rings the door bell, what do you do? Of course, you get up, and go to the door. Jesus was telling us that once we see all the signs converging on the world scene, AND we see Israel established as a nation, we are to **KNOW** that He is as close as the front door. In other words, it is time to get up, get ready, Jesus is ALMOST HERE!

WISE WILL UNDERSTAND

The book of Daniel ends with words that are prophetic for the time we now live:

"Go your way, Daniel, because the words are closed up and sealed UNTIL the TIME OF THE END. Many will be PURIFIED, made SPOTLESS and REFINED, but the wicked will continue to be wicked. None of the wicked will understand, but THOSE WHO ARE WISE WILL UNDERSTAND."

May Daniel's words reverberate in the reader's ears as they continue in this book. Many will be PURIFIED and made SPOTLESS and the WISE WILL UNDERSTAND.

CHAPTER 2

Escape Possible

Another clear indication we are nearing the return of the Lord, is the fact that the World is crying for Peace and Safety.

On September 27, 1991, President Bush announced a NEW ERA of "PEACE AND SECURITY" with sweeping nuclear arms reductions, as he took America off alert from possible attack from Russia.

The Middle East peace process began in October of 1991, and has progressed to the point that the parties are TALKING about PEACE and SECURITY.

The Apostle Paul warned us of this time:

"For yourselves know perfectly that the DAY OF THE LORD so cometh as a thief in the night [for the ungodly]. For when they shall **SAY**, PEACE and SAFETY, then sudden destruction cometh upon them, as travail upon a woman with child; and they shall not escape" (I Thessalonians 5:2-3, KJ).

Paul was telling us that there would come a time when the world would talk about PEACE and SAFETY. He was warning us that TALK is all it really is. The nations say they want peace, but we know that there will be no true peace until the "Prince of Peace," Jesus Christ returns.

Jeremiah reminds us: "Peace, peace, they say when there is no peace" (Jeremiah 6:14).

The main point needs to be understood that while they are **SAYING** PEACE and SAFETY, THEN sudden destruction will come. At some point, everyone will believe that peace has been achieved. When that point is reached, WATCH OUT! — for the Bible declares when they are saying peace and safety, then will come SUDDEN DESTRUCTION.

DAY OF THE LORD

This sudden destruction will usher in the time described in the Word of God, as the DAY of the LORD.

The Day of the Lord is a major doctrine that is referred to more than three hundred times in God's Word. For a more thorough description of this subject, please see the summary in Appendix C.

The Day of the Lord begins with the seven year Tribulation period, to be followed by the 1,000 years of peace during the reign of Christ. The Tribulation is the beginning of the Day of the Lord, and it will be one of the most horrible times for the inhabitants of the earth. It will be a time of testing and great trial. Revelation 6:8, indicates that one-quarter of the people will die. Of those remaining, Revelation 9:15, shows one-third of mankind will perish. Taken together, this tells us that one-half of the population of the earth will be destroyed during this awful time.

SHELTER POSSIBLE

While this coming period of destruction will be horrible for those left on the earth, the Word of God does indicate that there is a way of escape:

"The great day of the Lord is near, it is near, and hasteth greatly, even the voice of the day of the Lord: the mighty man shall cry there bitterly. That day is a day of wrath, a day of trouble and distress, a day of wasteness and desolation, a day of darkness and gloominess, a day of clouds and thick darkness, a day of trumpet and alarm against the fenced cities, and against the high towers" (Zephaniah 1:14-15, KJ).

"Before the decree bring forth, before the day pass as the chaff, before the fierce anger of the Lord come upon you, before the DAY of the LORD'S anger come upon you.

"SEEK ye the Lord, all ye meek of the earth, which have wrought his judgment; seek righteousness, seek meekness: *IT MAY BE* (or *PERHAPS*) ye SHALL BE HID IN THE DAY OF THE LORD'S ANGER" (Zephaniah 2:2-3, KJ).

The prophet Zephaniah indicated that some of those who are seeking the Lord, may be able to be hid from the horrible day of the Lord. He says to seek the Lord and **perhaps** you will be able to escape.

Notice that he does not indicate that you are definitely guaranteed of escaping. He uses the words *MAY BE* or *PERHAPS*, which would mean that not everyone will be able to escape.

LORD'S SAME TEACHING

Jesus confirms this same teaching for us:

"Watch, ye therefore, and pray always, that ye *MAY BE* ACCOUNTED WORTHY to escape all these things that shall come to pass, and to stand before the Son of man" (Luke 21:36, KJ).

Jesus told us to always pray that we *MAY BE* able to escape.

Jesus was telling this to His disciples. He is telling the Christian to pray that he is counted worthy of escaping the Tribulation period. This indicates that escape is possible, but is conditioned upon being accounted worthy in the Lord's eyes.

Both the prophet Zephaniah and the Lord show that escaping the Day of the Lord (or the Tribulation period) is possible. They both indicate that it is conditional and not something that is guaranteed or assured.

Jesus indicated that the Christians needed to pray that they may be accounted worthy in order to escape. This infers that not all Christians are automatically counted worthy. If they were, then Jesus would not have told us to pray such a prayer.

If all Christians were already guaranteed that they would escape the Tribulation period, then this instruction would be meaningless.

It is important to remember that we are not talking about salvation. We are talking about escaping the Tribulation. No one is worthy of salvation. We are saved completely by the grace of God:

> "For by grace are ye saved through faith; and that not of yourselves: it is the gift of God: Not of works, lest any man should boast" (Ephesians 2:8-9, KJ).

In the following chapter we will look further into what Jesus meant when He told us to pray that we are ACCOUNTED WORTHY of escaping the horrible Tribulation period.

CHAPTER 3

Counted Worthy to Escape

"Watch, ye therefore, and pray always, that ye MAY BE ACCOUNTED WORTHY to escape all these things that shall come to pass, and to stand before the Son of man" (Luke 21:36, KJ).

Jesus told us that we need to WATCH and PRAY ALWAYS that we are accounted WORTHY in order to escape the terrible Day of the Lord that will soon engulf this world. Escape is very possible, but it is also very conditional. It is not guaranteed or assured for any one. The Word of God makes it very clear that not all Christians are worthy and not all Christians will escape the Tribulation period.

WHO IS WORTHY

Revelation 3:4, tells us:

"Thou hast a FEW names even in Sardis which HAVE NOT DEFILED THEIR GARMENTS; and they shall walk with me in white: for they ARE **WORTHY**."

The second and third chapters of Revelation list seven churches which represent Christians. They are all believers in Christ, but only a FEW have the promise of escaping the

Tribulation period.

In Revelation 3:4, we see that the Church of Sardis had a FEW members who stood out from the rest. Overall, the Church of Sardis was dead; but it did have a FEW who were found WORTHY. They were found WORTHY because they had not defiled their garments.

Jesus is returning for His Bride. He expects her to be without spot or wrinkle and to be holy and without blemish (Ephesians 5:27).

While the Church of Sardis was dead, it did have a FEW members who had not defiled their garments. They had kept them spotless without any wrinkle or blemish. Because of this, they were considered **WORTHY.**

Remember that Jesus told us to pray that we are counted WORTHY to escape the Tribulation period. This picture of the FEW in Sardis shows us what it takes to be WORTHY.

Jesus is telling His Bride not to get her wedding garment dirty by this dark and dying world. To stay away from anything that would cause her to get her dress wrinkled or spotted. To keep herself separate from the things of this world and remain Holy and pure.

By so doing the Bride of Christ will be ready and found WORTHY when the Lord returns for her. As a result, she will be able to escape the Tribulation hour.

KEPT FROM TRIBULATION

Revelation also gives us another Church that is given the promise of escaping the horrible Tribulation period:

"Because thou hast KEPT THE WORD of my patience, I also will KEEP THEE FROM THE HOUR OF TEMPTATION (TRIBULATION), which shall come upon the world, to try them that dwell upon the earth" (Revelation 3:10, KJ).

This is the Church of Philadelphia. Because the members of this Church have KEPT GOD'S WORD, God promises to keep them out of the Tribulation period. This is also what James was trying to tell the Church:

"Do not merely listen to the Word, and so deceive yourselves. DO WHAT IT SAYS" (James 1:22).

By keeping God's Word, the Christian is given the promise of escaping the Tribulation hour. By not defiling their garment, the believer is considered worthy. By doing what the Word of God says and not soiling or wrinkling her wedding gown, the Bride of Christ can be confident that Jesus will take her to be with Him prior to when the Tribulation hour begins.

THOSE NOT WORTHY

The Word of God also describes a group of believers who are **NOT** considered **WORTHY:**

"The kingdom of heaven is like a king who prepared a wedding banquet for his son. He sent his servants to those who had been invited to the banquet to tell them to come, but they refused to come.

"Then he sent some more servants and said, 'Tell those who have been invited that I have prepared my dinner...and everything is ready. Come to the wedding banquet.'

"But they PAID NO ATTENTION TO IT [KJ: MADE LIGHT OF IT], and went off — one to his field, another to his business. . . .

"Then he said to his servants, 'The wedding banquet is ready, but those I invited did not deserve to come [KJ: were NOT WORTHY]' " (Matthew 22:2-5, and 22:8).

Because they did not pay attention to the invitation to come to the wedding banquet they missed out. The King James version says that they even made light of it. Because of their response, they are considered NOT WORTHY.

Earlier we showed that only those who are accounted worthy by the Lord, will be able to escape the Tribulation period. Since this group makes light of the message, they will find themselves in the Tribulation hour.

This is a parable for today's Christian. When the subject of the return of Christ is brought up, many Christians make light of it or pay no attention to it. They are too caught up with the things of this world to be concerned with thoughts of heaven. Because of their attitude, they are not considered WORTHY.

For a parallel passage to the above, the reader may want to study Luke 14:16-24. In Luke's version, everyone makes excuses on why they can not come to the wedding banquet. They were also caught up in the things of this world; and as a result, they made excuses and ended up missing the banquet.

In subsequent chapters we will discover that there are more references that show multitudes of Christians ending up in the Tribulation period. This is so unnecessary, because God does provide a way of escape. Those who are accounted worthy and who have not defiled themselves with this evil world, will be kept from the hour of testing that is coming to try this world. Escape is possible for those who are found worthy and looking for Him.

CHAPTER 4

Make Every Effort

We have seen that escaping the Tribulation period is not automatic or assured for any Christian. Only those who have, "KEPT THE WORD" and who have "NOT DEFILED THEIR GARMENTS" are given the blessed assurance of ESCAPING the Tribulation and being found WORTHY.

This implies that effort is required of the believer in order to escape the hour of trial. While salvation is a free gift that cannot be obtained by works (Ephesians 2:8-9), escape from the time of testing is based upon the merits of the individual believer's life.

MADE HERSELF READY

A good illustration of this is seen in the Bride of Christ:

"Hallelujah! For our Lord God Almighty reigns. Let us rejoice and be glad and give Him glory! For the wedding of the Lamb has come, and His **BRIDE HAS MADE HERSELF READY**" (Revelation 19:6-7).

Just as any earthly bride prepares for her wedding day, the Bride of Christ has to make preparations for her wedding to the Lamb of God. Effort is required in order to be ready. Further proof of this is seen in the verse which follows:

"Fine linen, bright and clean, was given her to wear."
(Fine linen stands for the righteous ACTS of the saints.)
(Revelation 19:8).

This indicates that the righteous ACTS of the believer is what provided the spotless wedding garment. Effort is required on the part of the believer if they want to have the fine linen that the Bride of Christ is wearing.

(The above translation of Revelation 19:8, is from the New International Version [NIV]. In this instance, it gives a truer rendering of the original Greek. Some will argue that the fine linen represents the righteousness that is imputed to the believer through Christ. This error helps foster the lukewarm attitude that will lead many Christians into the Tribulation period).

TEN VIRGINS

For further proof that effort is required, let's look at the parable of the ten virgins:

"At midnight the cry rang out: 'Here's the Bridegroom! Come out to meet him!' Then all the virgins woke up and trimmed their lamps. The foolish ones said to the wise, 'Give us some of your oil; our lamps are going out.'

" 'No,' they replied, 'There may not be enough for both us and you. Instead, go to those who sell oil and buy some for yourselves.' But while they were on their way to buy the oil, the bridegroom arrived. The virgins *WHO WERE READY* went in with him to the wedding banquet. And the door was shut" (Matthew 25:6-10).

Here we see that only the five wise virgins who were *READY* went into the wedding. The Greek for ready is: fit, prepared, or made ready.

While it appears the five foolish virgins were very busy, they were not properly prepared or ready when the bridegroom arrived. This is a picture of the Church today. Many appear to be very busy, but they are not making the proper preparations. They are not busy making themselves ready to meet their Bridegroom. We need to learn a lesson from the five wise virgins and prepare our lives to be ready to meet our Bridegroom: Jesus, when He returns for His Bride.

NECESSARY PREPARATIONS

In discussing prophecies concerning the end of time, Peter gives the Christian some very vital instruction:

> " . . . I have written . . . as reminders to stimulate you to wholesome thinking. Since everything will be destroyed in this way, what kind of people ought you to be? You ought to LIVE HOLY and GODLY LIVES as you look forward to the day of God and speed its coming. . . . So then, dear friends, since you are looking forward to this, *MAKE EVERY EFFORT* to be found SPOTLESS, BLAMELESS and AT PEACE with HIM." (II Peter 3:1, 11 & 14)

Peter tells us we need to MAKE EVERY EFFORT to be found BLAMELESS and to live HOLY and GODLY LIVES. This is further confirmation that effort is required by the believer. Jesus is coming for the believers who have made the necessary preparations. Those who are found SPOTLESS, BLAMELESS and at PEACE with Him will experience great joy at His return.

The Apostle Paul also taught us how we should be living when he was instructing the Church of the Thessalonians about the return of the Lord:

> "You are witnesses, and so is God, of how HOLY, RIGHTEOUS and BLAMELESS we were among you

who believed. For you know that we dealt with each of you as a father deals with his own children, encouraging, comforting, and URGING you to LIVE LIVES WORTHY OF GOD, who calls you into His kingdom and glory" (I Thessalonians 2:10-12).

"May he strengthen your hearts so that you will be BLAMELESS and HOLY in the presence of our God and Father when our Lord Jesus comes . . . " (I Thessalonians 3:13).

"Finally, brothers, we instructed you how to live in order to PLEASE God, as in fact you are living. Now we ask you and URGE you in the Lord Jesus to do this MORE and MORE" (I Thessalonians 4:1).

"For God did not call us to be impure, but to live a HOLY LIFE" (I Thessalonians 4:7).

Paul's instruction is vital to the Christian. God wants His children HOLY, PURE, RIGHTEOUS, and BLAMELESS. This type of life is necessary in order to be considered WORTHY. Paul was concerned that the BELIEVERS in the Church might not be found WORTHY. Notice his remarks in his second letter to this church:

"All this is evidence that God's judgement is right, and as a result you will be COUNTED WORTHY of the kingdom of God . . . " (II Thessalonians 1:5).

"With this in mind, we constantly pray for you, that our God MAY COUNT YOU WORTHY of His calling . . . " (II Thessalonians 1:11).

Paul knew the believer was not automatically COUNTED WORTHY before God. He URGED them to live their lives in such a way that God might find them properly prepared for the kingdom of God. He then relates that he constantly prayed for the believer's WORTHINESS! This sounds strikingly similar to the words the Lord told His disciples:

> "Watch, ye therefore, and pray always, that ye MAY
> BE ACCOUNTED WORTHY to escape all these things
> that shall come to pass, and to stand before the Son of
> man" (Luke 21:36, KJ).

It becomes abundantly clear that **WORTHINESS** before
the Lord is not a condition that is automatically bestowed upon
the believer at the time of salvation. If it were, Jesus and Paul
would not have stated prayer was needed to ensure the Christian
is found WORTHY.

UPWARD CALLING

Paul realized that being counted worthy before God was of
vital importance. He urged the disciples to live their lives in such
a way that they might be found acceptable before God, and he
prayed they might achieve this calling.

Remember that Paul was the believer who wrote the following words in Ephesians 2:8-9:

> "For by grace are ye saved through faith; and that not
> of yourselves: it is the gift of God: Not of works, lest any
> man should boast."

Paul knew that works played **no** part in his salvation. And
yet, Paul also wrote the following words, which indicate he was
very concerned about his own life:

> "That I may know Him, and the power of His
> resurrection, and the fellowship of His sufferings, being
> made conformable unto His death; **IF** BY ANY MEANS
> **I MIGHT** attain unto the resurrection of the dead.

> "Not as though I had already attained, either were
> already perfect: but I follow after, if that I may apprehend

that for which also I'm apprehended of Christ Jesus.

"Brethren, I count not myself to have apprehended: but this one thing I do, forgetting those things which are behind, and reaching forth unto those things which are before, I press toward the mark for the PRIZE of the HIGH CALLING of God in Christ Jesus" (Philippians 3:10-14, KJ).

Paul realized that his salvation did not guarantee that he would be found worthy to take part in the PRIZE of the HIGH CALLING. Paul knew that effort, on his part, was very necessary. He likened this quest to a race he was running, for which he knew had a very special prize.

He called this prize the HIGH CALLING. The meaning of the words in the original Greek is very interesting. High means UPWARD or ON THE TOP. Calling means INVITATION or calling. Paul might have been literally saying, "I press toward the mark for the prize of the UPWARD INVITATION or the TOP CALLING of God. . . . "

Paul's own striving for this special prize should be an example for every Christian to apply to their own life. Living in the final days of the Church age, the believer needs to heed Paul's instruction with utmost care. If we fail to hit the mark to which Paul says we need to strive, the consequences may be very grave. In subsequent chapters, we will see that this UPWARD CALLING is the promise of escaping the Tribulation period plus much more.

CHAPTER 5

First Fruit Believers

Many of the parables Jesus used were founded upon agricultural pictures, since the stories presented principles that were readily known and understood.

One of the best examples of this is found in the fourteenth chapter of Revelation. It describes the harvest of the earth; but more importantly, it gives an overall outline of the entire Tribulation period.

THE LAMB AND 144,000

This outline has been obscured from most in the Church because of the assumption that the 144,000 mentioned in Revelation 7:1-8, are the same 144,000 described in Revelation 14.

Those described in Revelation 7, are clearly servants of God from the 12 tribes of Israel. Note what is put on their foreheads:

"Do not harm the land or sea or the trees until we [angels] put a SEAL on the foreheads of the servants of our God. Then I heard the number of those who were sealed: 144,000 from all the tribes of Israel" (Revelation 7:3-4).

The 144,000 are sealed by God's angels as a protection from the wrath to come. The SEAL of protection is put in their foreheads.

Compare this to the foreheads of the 144,000 described in Revelation 14:1:

> "Then I looked, and there before me was the Lamb, standing on Mount Zion, and with him 144,000 who had **HIS NAME** and **HIS FATHER'S NAME** written on their foreheads."

These two groups of 144,000 clearly have different details written on their foreheads. The Jewish servants have SEALS, while the 144,000 in chapter 14, have the name of Jesus and the name of God written on theirs.

There are also other characteristics which show that these are not the same 144,000. Those in chapter 14 are in Heaven:

> "And I heard a sound from HEAVEN like the roar of rushing waters and like a loud peal of thunder. The sound I heard was like that of harpists playing their harps. And they sang a new song before the THRONE and before the four living creatures and the elders . . . " (Revelation 14:2-3).

Those found in Revelation 14, are in Heaven **_BEFORE_** the Tribulation begins (Revelation 14:6-7), while those described in Revelation 7:1-8, are sealed for protection from the wrath to come on the EARTH (see Revelation 9:4). The 144,000, of Revelation 7, are on the earth IN the Tribulation, while the scene shown in Revelation 14, is of 144,000, before the heavenly throne **_PRIOR TO_** the hour of Judgment.

This setting is also what is seen in Revelation 19:6:

> "After this I heard what sounded like a roar of a great multitude in HEAVEN shouting. . . .
>
> "Then I heard what sounded like a great multitude, like the roar of rushing waters and like loud peals of thunder shouting:

"Hallelujah! For our Lord God Almighty reigns. Let us rejoice and be glad and give him glory! For the wedding of the Lamb has come, and his Bride has made herself ready" (Revelation 19:1, 6-7).

Comparing Revelation 14 and 19, it is very clear the 144,000, that are described in chapter 14 are in fact in HEAVEN and not on the earth. For final proof this group is not the same as the 144,000 Jewish servants of chapter 7, notice the following:

". . . No one could learn the song except the 144,000 who HAD BEEN REDEEMED FROM THE EARTH" (Revelation 14:3).

This clearly identifies this group as an earthly remnant in heaven. They are 144,000 believers in Christ who have been TAKEN FROM the earth ***PRIOR TO*** the Tribulation. They are a very special group of people:

"These are those who did not DEFILE themselves with women, for they kept themselves PURE. They follow the Lamb wherever he goes. They were PUR-CHASED from among men and offered as FIRST FRUITS to God and the Lamb. No lie was found in their mouths; they are BLAMELESS" (Revelation 14:4-5).

Notice that this group had not DEFILED themselves, but were found PURE and BLAMELESS. This sounds strikingly similar to the description of those individuals revealed in the last two chapters. Those found worthy of escaping the Tribulation period:

Had not DEFILED THEIR GARMENT (Revelation 3:4).

Made every effort to be found SPOTLESS, BLAMELESS, and at PEACE with Him (II Peter 3:14).

Strengthened their hearts so they were found BLAMELESS and HOLY (I Thessalonians 3:13).

From the foregoing, it shows that this group of 144,000 represent Christians who had made the necessary preparations and were found worthy before God. Those found worthy of escaping the Tribulation hour were found BLAMELESS, SPOTLESS and UNDEFILED. Because of their PURE condition, they were taken to heaven as a FIRST FRUIT offering to God.

FIRST FRUITS

This select group of Christians was purchased from the earth as a **FIRST FRUITS** offering. The Greek for purchased means: to go to the market. It is a picture of God coming to the earth to select His FIRST FRUITS from the entire crop.

The farmer would gather the early crop as soon as enough had become ripe. Later, after the whole fields had been ripened by the summer heat, the entire crop would be harvested. The season would then close with the vintage, and the grapes were crushed in the vineyard.

This is a remarkable picture of what God is trying to reveal to us in Revelation 14. With the understanding that this group of 144,000 is not the same as the 144,000 given in Revelation 7, the picture of the entire period of the Tribulation hour becomes clear (please see Chart I).

PRE-TRIB & POST-TRIB CORRECT

Below is an outline of the entire Tribulation period as summarized in Revelation 14. It will be shown that both the pre-tribulation theory and the post-tribulation theory are partially correct. While both have parts that are right, they both have error that can cause the Christian great harm.

6 VISIONS OF REVELATION 14

1) FIRST FRUIT BELIEVERS — IN HEAVEN (verses 1-5)

2) HOUR OF JUDGEMENT HAS COME (verses 6-7)

3) BABYLON THE GREAT HAS FALLEN (verse 8)

4) PERSECUTION BY THE BEAST (verses 9-13)

5) JESUS RETURNS IN CLOUDS — FINAL HARVEST (verses 14-16)

6) VINTAGE — IN WINEPRESS OF GOD'S WRATH (verses 17-20)

Revelation 14, gives us a panoramic view of the entire Tribulation period. God placed this chapter immediately after the one that describes the reign of the two Beasts. It is, as if, God said, "Time out, let's look at this whole thing in perspective." And a beautiful perspective it is. Let's focus on the main points the end-time Christians need to understand.

First, God shows that **prior to** the Hour of Judgement, He plans to remove His FIRST FRUIT believers to Heaven. What a glorious hope this is to those living in these final days. As we have seen in previous chapters, God promises to take those believers who are accounted worthy, out of the Tribulation hour that is coming to test the whole world. After we are removed, judgement begins. This is precisely what is pictured in this summary chapter of Revelation 14.

Notice that God only removes the FIRST FRUIT believers. Not all Christians are taken at first. This is the major problem with the pre-tribulation view of the Rapture. It says that all Christians will be Raptured. God's Word reveals that only God's FIRST FRUITS are taken before the HOUR of JUDGEMENT begins.

This picture in Revelation 14, shows what has been discovered in previous chapters of this book. Escape from the Tribulation period is possible, but is conditional. It is not guaranteed for any Christian, but based upon the worthiness of each individual believer. Only those who are found BLAMELESS, SPOTLESS, and HOLY, and who have not DEFILED themselves, will be COUNTED WORTHY to be included in the Rapture of FIRST FRUIT BELIEVERS (see Question A — Appendix A).

After God removes His select group, He then allows Judgement to begin. Revelation 14, then reviews the two main episodes: the destruction of Babylon the Great, and the persecution by the Beast. Then the last two visions of Revelation 14, review the final gathering of the HARVEST and the VINTAGE.

HARVEST

When the Tribulation period is about over, the Lord Jesus Christ will return in the clouds:

> "I looked, and there before me was a white CLOUD. And seated on the CLOUD was one 'like a son of man' with a crown of gold on his head and a sharp sickle in his hand. Then another angel came out of the temple and called in a loud voice to him who was sitting on the CLOUD, 'Take your sickle and reap, because the time to reap has come, for the HARVEST of the earth is ripe' " (Revelation 14:14-15).

The Lord will return for the final HARVEST after the hour of Judgement has come to a close. This also agrees with the agricultural picture discussed earlier. The farmer gathered in his First Fruits from the early crop and then waited for the rest of the field to ripen at the end of the summer. When the summer was over, he would HARVEST the remainder of the crop.

VINTAGE

The final VINTAGE of the grape season is when the grapes are trodden down in the winepress. This is remarkably pictured as the final scene of Revelation 14:

> "The angel swung his sickle on the earth, gathered its grapes and threw them into the great winepress of God's wrath. They were trampled in the winepress outside the city, and blood flowed out of the press, rising as high as the horses' bridles for a distance of 1,600 stadia (180

miles)" (Revelation 14:19-20).

This sounds very similar to that final battle before the Millennium:

> ". . . He treads the winepress of the fury of the wrath of God Almighty" (Revelation 19:15).

Revelation 14 ends with the final battle of Armageddon. The chapter thus provides a very good summary or outline of the major events that are scheduled to occur during the period of the Tribulation. The Rapture of FIRST FRUIT believers is clearly indicated as the event that must precede this Tribulation hour. We will now discover just how these FIRST FRUIT believers arrived in heaven.

RIGHTLY DIVIDING THE WORD

The traditional verses used to show the Rapture are found in I Corinthians 15:51-52, and I Thessalonians 4:15-18. Later in this book, we will show that these verses will actually occur at the very end of the Tribulation period.

For all Pre-Tribulation followers, don't panic. There is still an escape before the Tribulation period begins. It has been there all along, but has been hidden. Remember that Paul taught us:

> "Study to show thyself approved unto God, a workman that needeth not to be ashamed, rightly dividing the word of truth" (II Timothy 2:15, KJ).

Most of the confusion over when the Rapture is to take place has resulted from the fact that we have not properly divided the Word of truth; and that includes this author, who asks for forgiveness. By following the various traditions that have been developed, we have all been lead astray from what God's wonderful Word has for us.

SNATCHED UP TO GOD

Chapter 12 of the book of Revelation tells us the story of a woman who gives birth to a male child. Most have incorrectly divided this section of the Word of truth, and said that this male child is Christ. By so doing, we have MISSED a vital KEY that reveals **WHEN** the Rapture takes place and **WHO** is actually taken in the Rapture. Let's see what we have been missing:

"A great & wondrous sign appeared in heaven:

"A woman clothed with the sun, with the moon under her feet and a crown of twelve stars on her head. She was pregnant and cried out in pain as she was about to give birth. Then another sign appeared in heaven: an enormous red dragon with seven heads and ten horns and seven crowns on his heads. His tail swept a third of the stars out of the sky and flung them to the earth. The dragon stood in front of the woman who was about to give birth, so that he might devour her child the moment it was born.

"She gave birth to a SON, a MALE CHILD, WHO WILL RULE ALL THE NATIONS WITH AN IRON SCEPTER.

"And her child was **SNATCHED UP** to God and to **HIS THRONE**" (Revelation 12:1-5).

This male child has been interpreted to be Jesus Christ. This is based upon Scriptures which do show that Jesus will rule the nations with a iron scepter:

"You will rule them with an iron scepter; you will dash them to pieces like pottery" (Psalm 2:8).

"Out of his mouth comes a sharp sword with which to strike down the nations. 'He will rule them with an iron scepter' " (Revelation 19:15).

It is clear that Jesus Christ will rule the nations with an iron scepter. But this is not enough evidence that the male child is in fact Jesus Christ.

Jesus Christ was born, then He DIED, and then He rose from the dead. This story of the male child shows him being born and THEN SNATCHED UP to the throne of God. If this child were Jesus Christ, it would have said that the dragon killed the child, and then the child was taken to the throne of God. It can be seen, from this, that the male child could not possibly be Jesus Christ. If it is not Jesus Christ, then who could it be? The Word of God beautifully answers this question for us, as we will see below.

OVERCOMERS

The book of Revelation gives many descriptions of those Christians that live exemplary lives before God. Jesus called them: OVERCOMERS:

"To him who OVERCOMES, I will give the right to eat from the tree of life, which is in the paradise of God" (Revelvation 2:7).

". . . He who OVERCOMES will not be hurt at the second death" (Revelation 2:11).

"To him who OVERCOMES, I will give some of the hidden manna. I will also give him a white stone with a new name written on it, known only to him . . . " (Revelation 2:17).

"To him who OVERCOMES will, like them (those few in Sardis who have not defiled their garments), be dressed in white . . . " (Revelation 3:5).

"Him who OVERCOMES I will make a pillar in the temple of my God. Never again will he leave it. I will write on him the *name of my God* and the name of the city of my God, the new Jerusalem, which is coming down out of heaven from my God; and I will also write on him *my new name*" (Revelation 3:12).

"To him who OVERCOMES, I will give the right to sit with me on my throne, just as I overcame and sat down with my Father on His throne" (Revelation 3:21).

"To him who OVERCOMES and does my will to the end, I will give authority over the nations — He WILL RULE THEM WITH AN IRON SCEPTER; HE WILL DASH THEM TO PIECES LIKE POTTERY" (Revelation 2:26 & 27).

As Christians, we are called to be OVERCOMERS. Not all Christians, however, are OVERCOMERS. Notice the description of the overcomers who are shown in the last listing: They will rule with Jesus Christ, "with AN IRON SCEPTER. . . . "

This is the precise description of the MALE CHILD, given in Revelation 12:5:

"She gave birth to a SON, a MALE CHILD, WHO WILL RULE ALL THE NATIONS WITH AN IRON SCEPTER.
"And her child was SNATCHED UP to God and to HIS THRONE."

The MALE CHILD will rule the nations with Jesus Christ with an IRON SCEPTER. This MALE CHILD is the Christian who is an OVERCOMER when Jesus returns to SNATCH him AWAY. He is the FIRST FRUIT believer that God will gather before His THRONE in heaven before the final harvest.

This male child is a select group of believers who will be taken to the throne of God in heaven before the dragon has a chance to kill him. The Christian who is an OVERCOMER and a FIRST FRUIT believer will be taken off of the earth to be with God before the devil has a chance to hurt him.

Notice how the Word of God beautifully connects the OVERCOMER with those believers who are assured of missing the Tribulation:

"To him who OVERCOMES and <u>DOES MY WILL</u> TO THE END . . . " (Revelation 2:26) COMPARED TO:

"Because thou hast <u>KEPT THE WORD</u> of my patience, I also will KEEP THEE FROM THE HOUR OF TEMPTATION . . . " (Revelation 3:10, KJ).

Those overcomers who DO God's WILL TO THE END or WHO KEEP God's WORD are given the blessed promise of being kept from going into the hour of testing.

Also, remember the *OVERCOMER* (Revelation 3:12) has the name of God and Jesus written on him. This harmonizes perfectly with the *FIRST FRUIT* believers described in Revelation 14:1. The FIRST FRUIT believer is the OVERCOMER who has the glorious assurance of not going into the Tribulation period. He is the MALE CHILD who is SNATCHED UP to the throne of God before the dragon can harm him (see Chart II for summary).

TAKEN OUT OF THE WAY

The above teaching is confirmed for us by Paul in his second letter to the Thessalonians. In this chapter, Paul discusses the timing of the Day of the Lord. He tells us:

"Let no man deceive you by any means: for that DAY [Day of the Lord] SHALL NOT COME, except there come a falling away first, and that man of sin [Anti-christ] be revealed, the son of perdition" (II Thessalonians 2:3, KJ).

He says that the falling away will precede the Day of the Lord. He also says that the Anti-christ will be revealed before that day comes. Notice, however, what is holding back the revelation of the Anti-christ:

"And now you know the thing holding back, for him to be revealed in his time. For the mystery of lawlessness already works, only HE holding back now, until it comes out of the midst; and then the Lawless One will be revealed . . . " (II Thessalonians 2:7-Interlinear translation).

This might be paraphrased: "He is holding the Anti-christ (who is already at work) from being revealed. When he is taken out of (or abundantly above) their midst, then the Anti-christ will be revealed."

Most have interpreted the "HE" in the above verses to represent the Holy Spirit. The theory states that the Holy Spirit is taken out through the Rapture of all Christians, and then the Anti-christ is revealed.

The problem with this theory, is the fact that the book of Revelation indicates that many people will be saved during the period of the Tribulation. If the Holy Spirit is taken out of their midst, it would be impossible for anyone to be saved after that.

The only possible explanation of who the "HE" is in the above verse, is the MALE CHILD that is found in Revelation 12:5. This fits in perfectly with what we have already learned. Once the MALE CHILD is taken out of the way (Greek: ABUNDANTLY ABOVE) then the Anti-christ is revealed. The MALE CHILD is SNATCHED UP to heaven, abundantly above, the reach of the dragon. Both are beautiful pictures of how God plans to keep this select group from the hands of Satan. Only after He has removed His select overcoming first fruit believers, will He allow the Anti-christ on stage.

CHART I

	144,000 JEWISH SERVANTS	144,000 FIRST FRUIT BELIEVERS
DIFFERENT FOREHEADS	Seal of Protection (Revelation 7:3)	Identification Mark (Revelation 14:1)
DIFFERENT LOCATIONS	On the Earth *during* the Tribulation (Rev. 7:3-4 & 9:4)	In Heaven *before* the Tribulation (Rev.14:1 & 14:7)
DIFFERENT PEOPLE	Tribes of Israel (Revelation 7:4)	Redeemed from the Earth (Rev. 14:3)
DIFFERENT ASSOCIATIONS	Living with Demon Locusts (Rev. 9:3-4)	Living with the Lamb Jesus (Rev. 14:1)

CHART II

	OVERCOMER	MALE CHILD	FIRST FRUIT BELIEVER
NAME ON FOREHEAD	"... I will write on him the *NAME of MY GOD* and ... *MY NEW NAME*" (Rev. 3:12).		"... 144,000 who had *HIS NAME* and *HIS FATHER'S NAME* written on their foreheads" (Rev. 14:1).
IRON SCEPTER	"To him who OVERCOMES ... he will *RULE THEM* with *AN IRON SCEPTER*" (Rev. 2:27).	"She gave birth to a **MALE CHILD**, who will *RULE THEM* with *AN IRON SCEPTER*" (Rev. 12:5).	
PRE-TRIB RAPTURE		"He was **SNATCHED UP** to God and to *HIS THRONE*" (Rev. 12:5).	"... 144,000 ... before the *THRONE* ... were redeemed from the earth" (Rev. 14:1-5).
UNDEFILED	"... a few names ... who have not *DEFILED* their garments ... they are worthy" (Rev. 3:4).		"... 144,000... these are they which were not *DEFILED* ..." (Rev.14:3 & 4).

CHAPTER 6

Spiritual Earthquake

The stage is being set for one of the most devastating earthquakes mankind could ever imagine. This is not an earthquake that will shake the earth's crust or even the economy. The earthquake that is coming is going to be a **SPIRITUAL EARTHQUAKE**.

Earthquakes are generally felt in one area of the world at any given point. The spiritual earthquake that is coming, will be felt around the world at the same time. It will be one of the most horrifying events in history.

The majority of Christians believe in the pre-tribulational theory of the Rapture. This theory states that ALL born-again believers will be taken in the Rapture, to be with the Lord, before the Tribulation period begins. Let's look at some of the major "fault-lines" in this widely accepted theory.

LAST TRUMPET

I Corinthians 15:51-52 are some of the main verses to show the pre-tribulational Rapture:

"Behold, I show you a mystery; We shall not all sleep, but we shall all be changed, in a moment, in the twinkling of an eye, at the **LAST TRUMPET**: for the trumpet shall sound, and the dead shall be raised incorruptible, and we shall be changed."

First of all, notice that Paul says the dead will be raised and the living changed at the **LAST TRUMPET**. When does the Word of God say the last trumpet will sound?

The book of Revelation answers this question for us. There are seven angels whose job it will be to sound seven trumpets. The angels begin in Revelation 8:6, and continue until the last one is sounded in Revelation 11. Notice the events surrounding the sounding of the seventh or LAST TRUMPET:

"The seventh angel sounded his trumpet, and there were loud voices in heaven, which said: 'The kingdom of the world has become the kingdom of our Lord and of his Christ, and he will reign for ever and ever.' (Christ's reign of the world begins.)

"And the twenty-four elders, who were seated on their thrones before God, fell on their faces and worshiped God, saying: 'We give thanks to you, Lord God Almighty, who is and who was, because you have taken your great power and HAVE BEGUN TO REIGN. The nations were angry; and your wrath has come. The TIME HAS COME for JUDGING the dead, and REWARDING your servants the prophets and your saints and those who reverence your name . . . ' " (Revelation 11:15-18).

The timing of the seventh trumpet or the **LAST TRUMPET** occurs when Jesus returns to the kingdom of the world to begin His reign. It is at this time that He will begin His judgement. This time was also prophesied by Enoch in Jude 14-15, KJ:

"And Enoch also, the seventh from Adam, prophesied of these, saying, Behold the Lord cometh with ten thousands of his saints, to execute judgement upon all. . . . "

Notice, it is at this time that Jesus returns with ten thousand of His saints to execute judgement. This is the return of the Lord at the very end of the Tribulation period. For further proof, the reader may want to read the description of Jesus Christ returning to the earth in Revelation 19:11-21.

The strong adherents to the pre-tribulation theory will argue that Paul said the last trumpet, but that it does not necessarily mean the last trumpet in the book of Revelation. While this argument has little basis, let's not argue; but let's look further into the words Paul used:

> "Behold, I show you a mystery; We shall not all sleep, but we shall all be changed, in a moment, in the twinkling of an eye, at the last trumpet: for the trumpet shall sound, and the DEAD SHALL BE RAISED incorruptible, and we shall be changed" (I Corinthians 15:51-52, KJ).

Notice that Paul says the DEAD SHALL BE RAISED at the sounding of the last trumpet. When will the dead be raised? The Word of God gives us a very clear answer with Daniel:

> "As for you [Daniel], go your way till the end. You will rest, and then AT THE END OF THE DAYS you WILL RISE to receive your allotted inheritance" (Daniel 12:12).

It is very clear that the dead will not rise until the very end of the days. The last trumpet will sound when the dead rise from their graves. This clearly places the **last trumpet** at the end of the Tribulation period. To argue that the last trumpet will sound before the end of the days is completely unfounded.

IN THE AIR

The other key verses that are used to show the pre-tribulational view are found in I Thessalonians 4:15-17:

"According to the Lord's own word, we tell you that we who are still alive, WHO ARE LEFT till the coming of the Lord, will certainly not precede those who have fallen asleep. For the Lord himself will come down from heaven, with a loud command, with the voice of the archangel and with the trumpet call of God, and the dead in Christ will rise first. After that, we who are still alive and WHO ARE LEFT will be caught up with them *IN THE CLOUDS* to meet the Lord in the air. And so we will be with the Lord forever."

Notice where the above event takes place. It says *IN THE CLOUDS*. This is the exact same place that was described in the previous chapter when the earth is HARVESTED:

"I looked, and there before me was a white CLOUD. And seated on the CLOUD was one 'like a son of man' with a crown of gold on his head and a sharp sickle in his hand. Then another angel came out of the temple and called in a loud voice to him who was sitting on the *CLOUD*, 'Take your sickle and reap, because the time to reap has come, for the HARVEST of the earth is ripe' " (Revelation 14:14-15).

This meeting in the CLOUDS takes place near the very end of the Tribulation period. Jesus is coming in the *CLOUDS* to gather in the whole HARVEST. This is the precise picture Paul was discussing in I Thessalonians 4. For further proof that this is so, notice the strong hint that Paul gave us in verses 15 and 17:

" . . . we tell you that we who are still alive, *WHO ARE LEFT* till the coming of the Lord. . . . "

" . . . After that, we who are still alive and *WHO ARE LEFT* will be caught up. . . . "

In both of these verses, Paul added the phrase: *WHO ARE LEFT*, or who remain. He could have just as easily left this out in both places. Unless...unless he was trying to convey something very important.

The Greek for this phrase is: to leave all around, survive, or remain. By adding this phrase in both places, Paul was trying to convey: some will remain, some will survive, some will be left all around. Paul was implying that some would be taken previously to the time mentioned, and that those who had not been taken, but *WHO REMAIN* will be taken at this time.

Through the Holy Spirit, Paul is implying that some will be taken earlier; and then those who were not taken earlier (but who remain) will be taken into the clouds to meet the Lord in the air.

This is precisely the scenario that has been developed thus far in this book. Some are taken in the Rapture of the First Fruit believers at first, followed by the final harvest of all who remain at the very end. The First Fruits are taken to the *throne* of God in *HEAVEN*, while the general harvest is gathered in by the Lord when He returns on the *CLOUDS* at the very end.

CRACKS IN THEORY

The pre-tribulation theory is largely based upon the scriptures that were outlined above. The pre-tribulational theory is believed by the majority of the Christian church and the majority of prophecy teachers and students.

We now see that there are some major cracks showing in this theory. These cracks can either be disregarded and ignored as utterly ridiculous, or they can be heeded by the leaders of the Church.

The severity of the COMING SPIRITUAL EARTHQUAKE

will be determined by the spiritual condition of each individual believer. The leaders of the Church will be held responsible for their condition.

When the Rapture of the First Fruit believers takes place; many Christians, who believed in the pre-tribulational Rapture, will be utterly devastated. The grief will be overwhelming. The horror of having to face the testing of the Tribulation period will be dreadful.

GREAT MULTITUDE

Most **WHO REMAIN** will be required to become martyrs for Christ. Some will be able to escape the wrath of the Anti-christ, but the majority will have to give up their life in order to reach heaven.

These facts are dramatically revealed to us in two places in Revelation:

> "After this I looked and there before me was a GREAT MULTITUDE that NO ONE COULD COUNT, from every nation, tribe, people and language, standing before the throne and in front of the Lamb.

> ". . . These are they who have COME OUT of the great tribulation; they have WASHED their ROBES and MADE them WHITE in the blood of the Lamb" (Revelation 7:9 & 14).

AND

> "They OVERCAME him [Anti-christ] by the blood of the Lamb and the word of their testimony; they did not love their lives so much as to shrink from death" (Revelation 12:11).

Notice the book of Revelation shows there will be a GREAT

MULTITUDE from every nation around the world. It will be a large group of people, too numerous to count. In all probability, this great multitude of born-again believers will be comprised of many of the Christians in our churches today.

SOILED ROBES

Notice that this group of Christians had to WASH their ROBES in order to make them WHITE. This tells us a great deal about them. First of all, it tells us that they had white robes at one time, which means that they were indeed Christians (Isaiah 61:10). Second, it tells us they somehow had gotten their robes dirty. This is a picture of the Christian too caught up with the things of this world. They had soiled their garments by not living the blameless, holy life they had been called to.

Remember those few in Sardis had not defiled their garments, and were able to walk with the Lord dressed in white because they were worthy. Had the great multitude heeded the Word of God, they would not have found themselves in the Tribulation period. They did not keep God's Word, and were not kept from the time of testing.

OVERCOMERS

Also notice this great multitude is finally required to become OVERCOMERS. In the last chapter, we saw that all Christians are called to be OVERCOMERS. Some were OVERCOMERS prior to the Tribulation period beginning. They were the First Fruit believers who had kept God's Word and kept themselves undefiled. They were found blameless, holy and worthy before God; thereby proving to be OVERCOMERS in God's sight.

The great multitude, on the other hand, will enter into the Tribulation period because they have not been true OVERCOMERS prior to when it begins. They will finally become OVERCOMERS when they are required to STAND UP for Christ during the Tribulation hour. Their only hope at that point, will be to die for Christ. They will have to refuse the mark of the beast and be martyred for Jesus.

SPIRITUAL EARTHQUAKE

Once the Rapture of First Fruit believers occurs, the Christians *remaining* will be completely surprised. Most had been taught all Christians are taken when the Rapture takes place. The horror of being left behind will be devastating. Blame, guilt and remorse will initially fill every believers heart. The true Church that remains will need to come together like it has never done before.

Until the SPIRITUAL EARTHQUAKE occurs, the believer still has time to prepare. This message is an exhortation to ALL born-again believers to repent and prepare to meet the Bridegroom. There is still time to be included in the First Fruits Rapture. There is still time to keep God's Word and be found holy, blameless, and worthy before God. Remember our Lord's instructions:

> *"Watch . . . and pray always, that ye may be accounted worthy to escape . . . "* (Luke 21:36).

CHAPTER 7

Upward Calling

In the fourth chapter we saw how the Apostle Paul was constantly striving for the PRIZE of the HIGH CALLING. This was seen in the verses which follow:

"That I may know Him, and the power of His resurrection, and the fellowship of His sufferings, being made conformable unto His death; IF BY ANY MEANS I MIGHT attain unto the resurrection of the dead.

"Not as though I had already attained, either were already perfect: but I follow after, if that I may apprehend that for which also I'm apprehended of Christ Jesus.

"Brethren, I count not myself to have apprehended: but this one thing I do, forgetting those things which are behind, and reaching forth unto those things which are before, I press toward the mark for the PRIZE of the HIGH CALLING of God in Christ Jesus" (Philippians 3:10-14, KJ).

Paul knew that he was saved by grace through faith in Jesus Christ. And yet, he knew that there was this HIGH CALLING to which he was not guaranteed.

As we have seen, the Greek for this high calling means: HIGH = UPWARD or ON THE TOP, and CALLING = INVI-

TATION or CALLING. Paul was seeking to obtain the upward invitation, or the top calling of God. He saw this as a prize to be won.

This is analogous to a runner in a race. Every participant strives to do their best in the hope of winning the top prize. No one is assured of that prize, and everyone strives to be the winner. In a race, there is always the possibility of stumbling or falling. The runner may not even be able to finish the race.

Paul recognized these possibilities, and tried to relay his sense of urgency to others. Notice his comments after talking about winning the prize:

> "All of us who are mature should take such a view of things. And if on some point you think differently, that too God will make clear to you" (Philippians 3:15).

Paul realized not everyone would understand the meaning of this upward calling; but he knew that they SHOULD if they were mature. He is saying that the mature Christian should understand this upward calling. If they don't understand, they should ask God to make it clear to them.

Just what is this upward calling which Paul so eagerly sought?

WORTHY OF THE KINGDOM

In an earlier chapter, we saw where Paul constantly prayed for the worthiness of his disciples. This was shown in the following Scriptures:

> "Which is the manifest token of the righteous judgement of God, that ye MAY BE COUNTED WORTHY of the KINGDOM OF GOD, for which ye also suffer" (II Thessalonians 1:5, KJ).

"Wherefore also we PRAY ALWAYS for you, that our God WOULD COUNT YOU WORTHY of this CALLING . . . " (II Thessalonians 1:11, KJ).

Paul knew that these disciples were indeed Christians. In fact, they were an exemplary Church (See I Thessalonians 1 and II Thessalonians 1:1-4). And yet, Paul constantly prayed that they may be counted worthy of the CALLING into the **KINGDOM OF GOD**. Although they were Christians, Paul constantly prayed that God might find them worthy of this calling.

Notice, Paul was also concerned about himself:

"That I may know Him, and the power of His resurrection, and the fellowship of His sufferings, being made conformable unto His death; IF BY ANY MEANS I MIGHT attain unto the resurrection of the dead" (Philippians 3:10 KJ).

Paul knew he was saved, and that his eternal destiny was secure. And yet, he indicates his own doubt about attaining to this resurrection of the dead. (The Interlinear translation reads: resurrection OUT OF the dead.)

Paul realized that his salvation did not assure him this. Because he was not sure, he pressed on, as if in a race, to win the prize. Paul knew there was a very special resurrection OUT OF the dead which he wanted to be counted worthy enough to participate in:

"Brethren, I count not myself to have apprehended: but this one thing I do, forgetting those things which are behind, and reaching forth unto those things which are before, I PRESS TOWARD THE MARK for the PRIZE of the HIGH CALLING of God in Christ Jesus" (Philippians 3:13-14, KJ).

Jesus also taught that there would be those who would be

WORTHY of this special calling which Paul so eagerly sought. This is found in Luke 20:35:

> "But those who are considered WORTHY of taking part in THAT AGE and in the resurrection from the dead. . . . "

Jesus indicated that there would be a special group that would be considered WORTHY enough to participate in this resurrection from the dead. But notice He also indicated they would take part in a certain AGE. The Greek shows that this is a Messianic period or an age.

1,000 YEAR REIGN

The first resurrection begins a period of 1,000 years. This is described in the book of Revelation:

> "BLESSED and HOLY is he that hath part in the first resurrection: on such the second death hath no power, but they shall be priests of God and of Christ, and shall reign with Him a thousand years" (Revelation 20:6, KJ).

This indicates that those who take part in the first resurrection are considered BLESSED and HOLY. This shows it is for a special group of people. Could it be those who are considered WORTHY in God's sight? Let's see who is included in this first resurrection from the dead:

> "I saw (1) thrones on which WERE SEATED those who had been given authority to JUDGE. AND I saw (2) the SOULS of those who had been beheaded because of their testimony for Jesus and because of the Word of God. They had not worshiped the beast or his image and had not received his mark on their foreheads or their hands. They came to life and reigned with Christ a thousand years" (Revelation 20:4).

Notice there are two groups in view here. The second group John saw were the SOULS who had been martyred for Jesus. Notice that only the SOULS were seen at first, and THEN they came to life to reign with Christ for 1,000 years. This places the first resurrection near the very beginning of the Millennium.

This second group represents those who died for Jesus during the Tribulation period. They are given the honor of reigning with Christ during the Millennium because of this.

The first group consists of those who were seated on thrones with the authority to judge. We know from I Corinthians 6:2, the saints are the ones who will judge the world. In the above scene, however, notice where this group is located. It says: **seated on thrones**.

We saw earlier in this book, the OVERCOMERS are the ones who are seated on the throne with God:

> "To him who OVERCOMES, I will give the right to SIT with me on my THRONE, just as I overcame and sat down with my Father on His throne" (Revelation 3:21).

Only the OVERCOMERS are given the right to sit on the throne of God. The group in view at the first resurrection includes those who were overcomers prior to when the Tribulation period began, plus those who through martyrdom became overcomers by the word of their own testimony (Revelation 12:11).

The timing and purpose of this scene is also verified by Jude 14:

> "And Enoch also . . . prophesied of these, saying, Behold, the Lord cometh with ten thousands of his saints, to execute judgement upon all . . . " (Jude 14, KJ).

The first group mentioned as part of the first resurrection, represent the overcoming saints of God who will be given thrones from which they will have the authority to judge. While all saints are called to judge the world, only those who were overcomers are seen as part of the first resurrection.

BOOK OF LIFE

If all saints are to judge the world, and only the overcomers and martyrs are included in the first resurrection, then when are the rest of the saints raised?

The only possible explanation is that they are resurrected at the end of the 1,000 year Millennium. This is described for us in Revelation 20:7, 11-15, KJ. Pay particular attention to the last verse:

"And when the thousand years are expired, Satan shall be loosed out of his prison. . . .

"And I saw a great white throne, and him that sat on it, from whose face the earth and the heaven fled away; and there was found no place for them. And I saw the dead, small and great, stand before God; and the books were opened: and another book was opened, which is the BOOK OF LIFE: and the dead were judged out of those things which were written in the books, according to their works.

"And the sea gave up the dead which were in it; and death and hell delivered up the dead which were in them: and they were judged every man according to their works:

"And **WHOSOEVER** was **not** found written in the BOOK OF LIFE was cast into the lake of fire."

The last verse indicates that WHOSOEVER was not included in the book of life, was thrown into the lake of fire. This *implies* that there will be some at the end of the 1,000 years who will be present whose names ARE found written in the BOOK

OF LIFE.

This group of people must represent all those true born-again believers who were not found part of the first resurrection. Although they missed the 1,000 year reign with Christ, their names were found written in the book of life, and they were not thrown into the lake of fire.

These Christians were indeed saved, and their names could never be erased from the book of life. They missed the Rapture of First Fruit believers because they were not considered worthy. Once they entered into the Tribulation period they could have participated in the first resurrection by becoming martyrs. The fact they did not become martyrs indicates they must have died before they had a chance to be martyred. This is highly probable, knowing that over 3 billion people will die during the Tribulation period.

EXCLUDED FROM THE KINGDOM

The Word of God does indicate that there will be Christians who do not enter into this 1,000 year reign with Christ:

> "Not everyone who says to me, 'Lord, Lord,' will enter the KINGDOM OF HEAVEN, but only he who does the will of my Father who is in heaven" (Matthew 7:21).

The fact these people called Jesus 'Lord' indicates that they were Christians (please see I Corinthians 12:3). This indicates that there will be Christians who will not enter into the 1,000 year reign with Christ, known as the KINGDOM OF HEAVEN. This is that HIGH or UPWARD calling which Paul so fervently sought.

Many of the other parables Jesus taught, also indicate there will be some Christians who are excluded from reigning with Christ during the Kingdom. The reader may want to read:

Matthew 25:1-30; and Luke 13:22-30; for examples of this teaching. Please keep in mind that exclusion from the Kingdom does not mean exclusion from Heaven.

WORTHY OF UPWARD CALLING

Remember that Jesus taught there are those who are considered worthy of participating in the kingdom age:

> "But those who are considered WORTHY of taking part in THAT AGE and in the resurrection from the dead . . . " (Luke 20:35).

There is a group of believers God considers worthy of participating in the future kingdom during the Millennium. This is a select group of born-again believers who please God.

Also remember those who take part in this resurrection are called: "BLESSED and HOLY" (see Revelation 20:6). These words were written by the Apostle John. One of his disciples was named Polycarp, who contributed the following to this subject:

> "**If** we please Him in this present age, we shall also receive the Age to Come; and **if** we walk worthy of Him, we shall also reign together with Him."

Polycarp's insight seems to parallel what has been brought out in this book. Those who please God by living holy and blameless lives in this present time, will be found worthy of the wonderful privilege of reigning with Christ during the 1,000 year Millennium.

UPWARD CALLING

Those first fruit believers who are overcomers will be considered blessed and holy and worthy to take part in the first resurrection and the 1,000 year reign with Christ.

While the first resurrection will include both the first fruit overcomers and the martyrs of the Tribulation period, the HIGH CALLING is to be included in the first fruit group, and thereby escape the Tribulation entirely. Both are included in the first resurrection, but the former group represents the UPWARD CALLING which Paul so fervently sought.

The value of praying the way Jesus taught us to pray, brings on added importance:

> "Watch ye therefore, and pray always, that ye may be accounted worthy to escape all these things that shall come to pass, and to stand before the Son of man" (Luke 21:36, KJ).

By praying the above prayer, with a heartfelt desire, God will provide a way for those who are truly sincere and committed to His Word. By the power of His Spirit, they will be able to escape the Tribulation and be automatically included in the first resurrection. To be included is truly the UPWARD CALLING all should earnestly strive and pray.

CHAPTER 8

Timing of First Coming

One of the greatest Prophecies in the Word of God is the prophecy surrounding the first coming of our Lord Jesus Christ. Books have been written about the extraordinary way in which God fulfilled His Word to the precise moment in history.

The main prophecy we will be looking at is found in Daniel 9:24-26, KJ:

"Seventy weeks [70-7's] are determined upon thy people [Israel] and upon thy holy city, to finish the transgression, and to make an end of sins, and to make reconciliation for iniquity, and to bring in everlasting righteousness, and to seal up the vision and prophecy, and to anoint the most Holy.

"Know therefore and understand, that from the going forth of the commandment to RESTORE and BUILD JERUSALEM unto the Messiah the Prince shall be seven weeks [49 years], and threescore and two weeks [434 years or a total of 483 years]: the street shall be built again, and the wall, even in troublous times.

"And after threescore and two weeks shall Messiah be cut off, but not for himself. . . . "

Daniel was given a prophecy as to the exact timing of when

the Messiah would arrive on the scene. Had the religious leaders and students of the Word of God properly "divided the Word of Truth," they would have been able to determine when Jesus was predicted to come and the timing of when He was to be "cut off" or killed.

In Daniel 9:24, it says that seventy weeks are determined upon the people Israel. In the original Hebrew this reads seventy sevens. In other words, seventy sets of seven years, or 490 years are determined upon Israel. It says that when this period of 490 years are complete, there will come an end to sin and everlasting righteousness will be brought forth. What a glorious day that will be!

483 YEARS FULFILLED

Of the total of 490 years decreed upon Israel, only 483 years have been fulfilled. Of the total 70 weeks of Daniel, only 69 weeks have been accomplished. This can be illustrated as follows:

COMPLETED

7 Weeks	x	7	=	49 Years
62 Weeks	x	7	=	434 Years
69 Weeks				483 Years

+ REMAINING

1 Week	x	7	=	7 Years

TOTAL

70 Weeks		490 Years

Now let's look at the starting point for this amazing prophecy. Notice that it says:

"Know therefore and understand, that from the going forth of the commandment to RESTORE and BUILD JERUSALEM . . . " (Daniel 9:25).

The point this prophecy is to begin from is the commandment to restore Jerusalem. This date is found in Nehemiah 2:

"In the month of Nisan in the twentieth year of King Artaxerxes. . . .

" . . . I went to the governors . . . and gave them the king's letters. The king had also sent army officers and cavalry with me. . . .

" . . . Come, let us rebuild the wall of Jerusalem. . . . Let us start rebuilding . . . " (Nehemiah 2:1, 9, 17-18).

The reader may want to read the entire second chapter of Nehemiah for an overview. In it you will see that the King gave Nehemiah the letters or the "commandment" to rebuild the city of Jerusalem in the month of Nisan in the twentieth year of his reign.

This places the starting point for Daniel's prophecy at Nisan 445 B.C. According to astronomical records the 1st of Nisan in that year would have been on March 14, 445 B.C.

Now, let's see how many years we are to count from this decree to rebuild Jerusalem:

" . . . (from) the commandment to restore and build Jerusalem unto the Messiah the Prince shall be seven weeks [49 years], and threescore and two weeks [434 years]: [or a total of 483 years]" (Daniel 9:25, KJ).

Daniel says it will be a total of seven weeks and sixty-two weeks. Added together, this is a total of 69 weeks of years. Sixty-nine times seven equals 483 years. After these 483 years, Daniel says that the Messiah will be "cut off, but not for himself. . . . "

In other words, after the 483 years had transpired, He was to be crucified for mankind.

PROPHETIC TIME

In calculating this prophecy, we need to take into account how Daniel would have measured the length of a year. In the account of the Flood we are told there were 150 days from the 17th day of the second month, until the 17th day of the seventh month (Genesis 7:11 & 8:3). This tells us that each month would be 30 days long (30x5=150).

Based upon this line of reasoning, a year in God's prophetic timetable would be: 12 months times 30 days, or 360 days long.

We know that Daniel said there would be 483 years from the time that the decree to rebuild Jerusalem until the Messiah was "cut off." We now need to convert these 483 solar years into 483 prophetic years as follows:

$$483 \times 360 \quad = \quad 173,880 \text{ days}$$

$$\frac{173,880}{365.25} \quad = \quad 476.1 \text{ years}$$

This is saying there would be approximately 476 prophetic years in 483 solar years. When Daniel said there would be 483 years from the time the commandment to rebuild Jerusalem until Jesus is cut-off, he was speaking in terms of a prophetic year that is 360 days long. The conversion that is outlined above, takes these 483 solar years and equates them with 476 prophetic years.

Now let's move forward 476.1 prophetic years from March 14, 445 B.C.:

Rebuild Jerusalem	March 14, 445 B.C.
+ 476 Prophetic years	476.1
Time Jesus Cut Off	April 6, 32 A.D.

In the above calculation, it needs to be remembered that there is no year between 1 B.C. and 1 A.D.:

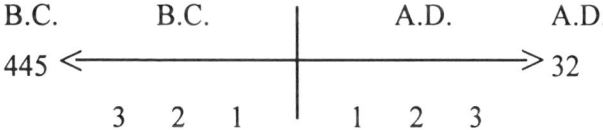

What the above calculations reveal is truly amazing! Daniel's prophecy concerning Israel and her Messiah <u>showed the exact date</u> that Jesus was to be cut off. Had the religious students studied this prophecy, they would have been able to know their Messiah was present!

OTHER POSSIBILITIES

Some argue that the commandment to rebuild Jerusalem was not in 445 B.C. By using other dates for this decree, they arrive at varying dates for the time Jesus was crucified. These range from 30 A.D. to 33 A.D.

For purposes of this book, the point becomes immaterial. By focusing on the year, we can miss the significance of Daniel's prophecy.

One of the reasons Daniel was given this prophecy, was to reveal to Israel the exact time that their Messiah would arrive on the scene and the time He would be cut off.

Had the people diligently studied God's Word they would have been able to perform the same calculations as we have done in this chapter. From their own records, they would have been able to determine the exact moment Jesus was to be present and the time he was to be cut off.

They could have known and THEY SHOULD HAVE KNOWN when their Messiah was to arrive. By failing to read and study God's Word, they missed the First Coming of Jesus Christ!

STUDY TO BE APPROVED

The New Testament believers are given the following admonition in II Timothy 2:15, KJ:

> "Study to show thyself approved unto God, a workman that needeth not to be ashamed, rightly dividing the Word of Truth."

Had the Old Testament believers rightly divided God's Word, they would not have crucified their Messiah. As a result of not heeding the Scripture, they will be ashamed when He returns and they will mourn when they recognize who they had pierced:

> ". . . They will look on me, the one they have pierced, and they will mourn for him as one mourns for an only child, and grieve bitterly for him as one grieves for a first-born son" (Zechariah 12:10).

May God use the example of the Old Testament believers to teach the end-time New Testament believers to take God's Word seriously. As born-again believers living near the time when Jesus Christ is returning, we need to study God's Word. We need to diligently search the Scriptures, with the aid of the Holy Spirit, to make sure that we are not ashamed. We need to heed God's Word and study it with a burning desire to know all God wants us to know.

PROPER HEART

The First Coming of Jesus Christ was predicted by Daniel. Had the religious leaders and students of God's Word studied this prophecy with the proper heart, they could have been in a position to welcome their Messiah instead of crucifying Him.

The Second Coming of Jesus Christ is rapidly drawing near. May we learn from the mistakes of the past, and study God's Word with a proper heart. May we heed God's Word and be in a position to welcome Jesus when He returns.

CHAPTER 9

Timing of Second Coming

In the first chapter, we saw that the wise and faithful servant of Jesus Christ will know the time when He returns and will be looking for Him. In I Thessalonians 5:4, Paul even said that the Christian is not in darkness, so that it SHOULD NOT take them by surprise.

We have just seen, in the previous chapter, that the religious leaders and students of God's Word should have been able to calculate the exact moment when their Messiah would arrive. Remember how Jesus rebuked them:

"When it is evening ye say, 'It will be fair weather; for the sky is red.' And in the morning, 'It will be foul weather today: for the sky is red and lowring.' O YE HYPOCRITES, ye can discern the face of the sky; but can ye not discern the SIGNS OF THE TIMES?" (Matthew 16:2-3, KJ).

We need to take our Lord's words to heart. All of the signs Jesus told us about are being fulfilled in the daily news. Israel is back in her land and the Middle East peace process shows signs that we may not be far away from a peace treaty. Let's not be like those who missed Jesus when He returned the first time. Let's consider what the Word of God has to say regarding the timing of His Second Coming.

DATE SETTING

The purpose of this chapter is **NOT** to set a date for the Rapture of First Fruit believers. While a specific date will not be set, we will consider several possibilities as to the timing of end-time events. Remember that Jesus even commanded us to KNOW when His return was near:

"So likewise ye, when ye shall see all these things, KNOW THAT IT IS NEAR, EVEN AT THE DOORS" (Matthew 24:33, KJ).

Since we are to **KNOW** when it is near, we should be diligently seeking the Word of God for clues and evidence of His return.

KINGDOM NEAR

In the above verse we see that Jesus says "IT" is near. What does He mean by this?

The answer is found in the parallel passage recorded in Luke 21:31, KJ:

"So likewise ye, when ye see these things come to pass, KNOW ye that the KINGDOM OF GOD is nigh at hand."

Jesus is telling the Christian to know that the KINGDOM OF GOD is near. This is the 1,000 year Millennium that was discussed in previous chapters. It is the 1,000 year reign with Jesus Christ that begins right after the end of the horrible Tribulation period. Before the Kingdom is brought to this earth, the world will undergo this terrible time of testing. This can be shown in the following diagram:

CHURCH AGE (AGE OF GRACE)	TRIBULATION (TEST)	MILLENNIUM (KINGDOM AGE)
(2,000? Years)	(7 Years)	(1,000 Years)

GENERATION WILL NOT PASS AWAY

Right after Jesus told us we are to know that the Kingdom is near, He gives us one of the biggest clues as to WHEN it will occur:

"Verily I say unto you, This generation shall not pass, till all these things be fulfilled" (Matthew 24:34, KJ).

Jesus says, THIS generation will not pass until all these things have happened. From previous verses we know that the generation He was talking about is the generation that witnessed the "fig tree" blossom. This was discussed in the first chapter, where we saw that Israel is the fig tree. Israel became a nation on May 14, 1948, and was recognized by the United Nations on May 15, 1949. Jesus said that the generation which is alive to see this happen **will not pass away**.

Notice that Jesus says this generation will not pass away until all of "these things be fulfilled." Here He is referring to all of the things He had discussed earlier. This included: wars, rumors of wars, earthquakes, famines, etc. He was also saying that this generation would not pass away until:

" . . . They will see the Son of Man coming on the clouds of the sky, with power and great glory" (Matthew 24:30).

In other words, the generation that is alive to witness Israel established as a nation will not pass away until it has seen Jesus

Christ returning on the clouds! This event with Jesus coming on the clouds is His Second Coming at the very end of the Tribulation period. The generation to witness Israel reborn will also witness the Second Coming of Jesus Christ!

LENGTH OF GENERATION

The question this raises is: How long is the generation Jesus was referring to?

Many felt the length of this generation was 40 years long. The Word of God does reveal the number 40 is related to a time of testing. Many added 40 to 1948, and said that the Lord was going to return in 1988. Now that we are past this time, we should look further into the Word of God for other possibilities.

STARTING POINT

The correct starting point for the length of the generation could be either (1) May 14, 1948 or (2) May 15, 1949.

On May 14, 1948, Israel declared itself as a nation. This could be the starting point to measure the generation that will see the Second Coming.

The other possibility is May 15, 1949. On this day Israel was formally recognized by the United Nations. In Numbers 23:9, the Prophet Balaam predicted a time when Israel: " . . . shall not be reckoned among the nations." Indeed, Israel was not "reckoned" by the nations until May 15, 1949, when Israel was finally recognized by the United Nations.

42 GENERATIONS

An interesting insight was recently brought out by a leading prophecy teacher. He may have actually discovered the length of a generation. In Matthew 1:1-17 it lists the genealogy from Abraham to Jesus Christ. This represents 42 generations over

2,166 years. Dividing 2,166 by 42 tells us the length of the average generation from Abraham until Christ's First Coming was 51.57 years. We can not be 100% certain that this is the length of the generation Jesus was referring to in the parable of the fig tree. We were told by the Lord to LEARN A LESSON from this parable. All good teachers know that if students don't try, they will never learn anything. Let's see where this answer of 51.57 years leads us.

Using May 15, 1949 as a starting point, we need to add 51.57 years. This would end in the year 2,000. In other words, if the length of the generation Jesus was referring to is to be approximately 51.57 years long, that generation would end around the year 2,000. This would indicate that the Second Coming of Jesus would have to occur around the year 2,000, since Jesus said that this generation would live to see His return.

7 YEAR TRIBULATION

We saw in the last chapter where God still has a 7 year period of time remaining that He plans to deal with the nation of Israel. This is the 70th Week of Daniel or the seven year Tribulation period. We need to subtract this time from the time of the Second Coming because the Rapture of the First Fruit believers occurs prior to when the Tribulation period begins.

Subtracting 7 years from the year 2,000, and we arrive at 1993. According to this rather easy calculation, the Rapture of the First Fruit believers **COULD** occur in 1993:

$$1949 + 51.57 \text{ years} = 2,000 - 7 \text{ years} = 1993$$

TWO DAYS OR 2,000 YEARS

In the previous chapter we saw how God gave mankind a prophecy that pinpointed the exact time of the Lord's First Coming. Let's use the same methodology to see if the Word of God gives further clues to His Second Coming.

In Hosea 6:2, God says He will restore Israel to live in His presence after two days or 2,000 years of time. After the 6,000 years of mankind are ended, God will usher in the final Millennial Kingdom:

ADAM TO CHRIST	JESUS COMING	KINGDOM AGE
1ST		2ND
(4,000 Years)	(2,000Yr)	(1,000Yr)

The question becomes: How do we calculate the 2,000 years between His First and Second Comings and what is the correct starting point?

Remember in the last chapter we needed to convert Daniel's 483 Solar years into 476 Prophetic years. This is because it was shown that God uses a 360 day year instead of a 365 day year to measure time.

Let's convert these 2,000 years into Prophetic years:

$$2,000 \times 360 = 720,000 \text{ days}$$

$$\frac{720,000}{365.25} = 1971.25 \text{ years}$$

The above calculation is telling us that there are 1,971.25 Prophetic years in the 2,000 Solar years. This is the exact same method that we used in the previous chapter which yielded an answer to the precise moment of when Jesus Christ was cut off.

If this is the correct calculation, it is telling us that there are only 1,971.25 years from some point until the beginning of the Millennium Kingdom. But what is the starting point we should use?

RESTORE US

Let's remember what Hosea 6:2, says:

"After two days he will revive us; on the third day he will restore us, that we may live in his presence."

This is a prophecy for the restoration of Israel. After the two days or 2,000 years are completed, He will restore Israel so they may live in the Lord's presence in the third day; ie., the 1,000 year Millennium.

Does the Word of God give us any indication as to when Israel officially rejected their Messiah? Of course, the Crucifixion of Jesus comes to mind; but was there an earlier time that Israel rejected Jesus?

ACCEPTABLE YEAR

Right after Jesus was baptized and tempted in the wilderness, He began His ministry in the synagogue with the following sermon:

"The Spirit of the Lord is upon me, because he hath anointed me to preach the gospel to the poor; he hath sent me to heal the broken-hearted, to preach deliverance to the captives, and recovering of sight to the blind, to set at liberty them that are bruised, to preach the ACCEPTABLE YEAR of the Lord" (Luke 4:18-19, KJ).

Jesus read this from the prophet Isaiah. After he finished reading the above, He closed the book and said to those present:

". . . This day is this Scripture FULFILLED in your ears."

Jesus was telling them the ACCEPTABLE YEAR of the

Lord was FULFILLED on that very day. When the people in the synagogue heard this, they were furious. They drove Jesus out of town and even attempted to throw Him off a cliff.

On the very day that Jesus proclaimed the acceptable year of the Lord, Israel rejected their Messiah. This day marked the beginning of Israel turning from their promised one. Instead of acknowledging the Lord, Israel rejected the one who could restore them.

It is very possible that this is the correct starting point for the prophecy in Hosea. The main point of Hosea's prophecy is the restoration of Israel. That day in the synagogue marked a turning point for Israel. Had Israel acknowledged Jesus, He could have restored them at that time. Because Israel rejected their Messiah, restoration of Israel was postponed for 2,000 years.

MINISTRY BEGAN IN 29 A.D.

If this sermon is the correct starting point, then when did Jesus give it?

The best evidence shows that Jesus began His ministry in 29 A.D. Jesus probably delivered His sermon in the synagogue in the early part of 29 A.D. If 29 A.D. is the correct starting point, let's see where this leads us:

Israel rejected Jesus	29 A.D.
+ 1,971 Prophetic Years	1971 Years
Second Coming	2000 A.D.
- Tribulation Period	7 Years
First Fruits Rapture	1993 A.D.

Moving forward 2,000 Solar years, which translates into 1,971 Prophetic years, we arrive at the year 2000 A.D. as the possible time for the Second Coming of Jesus Christ. This would be the time that Israel would be restored to live in the presence of their Messiah. This is exactly what the prophet Hosea was saying. After two days or 2,000 years the Lord would restore Israel.

If the Second Coming of Jesus is to be in the year 2000 A.D., then the Rapture of the First Fruit believers would occur seven years earlier, or in 1993. This is the same time we arrived at in the first part of this chapter.

Both methods come directly from the Word of God. The first one is a calculation of the "fig tree" generation, while the second one is a calculation of an Old Testament prophecy using the same methodology that was used in arriving at the timing of His First Coming. Both confirm that 2000 A.D. could be the time of His Second Coming, and 1993, as the time of the Rapture of First Fruit believers.

As was stated earlier, the purpose of this chapter is **NOT** to set a date for the Rapture of First Fruit believers. Because we know that we are living in the generation that Jesus said would witness His Second Coming, we would be slothful if we did not diligently seek His Word for clues to when it might be.

We need to remember that His First Coming was missed because of the attitude of the people. Let's not miss the timing of His Second Coming and Rapture for failure to discern the signs of the time and the signs given in the Word of God.

SEE THROUGH GLASS DARKLY

Thus far, we have seen that there is very good evidence that the Second Coming could occur in the year 2000 A.D., with the Rapture of First Fruit believers occurring seven years earlier in 1993. While we cannot be dogmatic about these dates, the First Fruit believer will be looking for her Bridegroom with an extra sense of joy and expectancy in the hope that these calculations are correct.

Paul reminded us in I Corinthians 13:12, KJ:

"For now we see through a glass, darkly; but then face to face: now I know in part; but then shall I know even as I am known."

As diligently as we try, we cannot know for certain. Now we only know in part. We may make mistakes along the way, but the Lord knows our hearts. Sometimes our desire to be with Him, can fog the glass, and cause us to make errors in our interpretations.

While the First Fruit believer will hope the above interpretations are correct, let's look at some other possibilities as to the timing of end-time events.

OTHER POSSIBILITIES

2000 Prophetic Years

In our interpretation of Hosea 6:2, we used the beginning of our Lord's ministry, 29 A.D. as the starting point. While this appears to be a sound basis for analyzing this prophecy, there is one other possibility. The ultimate rejection by Israel of their Messiah occurred at the Crucifixion of Jesus. As was noted previously, the exact timing of this event varies between 30 A.D. to 33 A.D., with the most widely accepted date being 32 A.D. Let's use 32 A.D. as our starting point to see where this leads us:

Israel crucified Jesus	32 A.D.
+ 1,971 Prophetic Years	1971 Years
Second Coming	2003 A.D.
- Tribulation Period	7 Years
First Fruits Rapture	1996 A.D.

If 32 A.D. is the correct starting point, the Second Coming of Jesus could occur in the year 2003 A.D., with the Rapture of First Fruit believers seven years prior in 1996.

Fig Tree Generation

In our interpretation of the parable of the "fig tree" we used 51.57 years as the length of a generation. This was arrived at through the length of the 42 generations from Abraham until the First Coming of Christ. While this is believed the correct interpretation, let's see if there are other possibilities.

Psalm 90:10, tells us:

> "The length of our days is seventy years — or eighty, if we have the strength; yet their span is but trouble and sorrow, for they quickly pass, and we fly away."

Psalm 90, could be telling us that the length of a generation is 70 to 80 years long. If this is the length of the generation of the "fig tree" we arrive at the following results:

Israel recognized by U.N.	1949 A.D.
+ Generation - Psalm 90	70 Years
Second Coming	2019 A.D.
- Tribulation Period	7 Years
First Fruits Rapture	2012 A.D.

OR

Israel recognized by U.N.	1949 A.D.
+ Generation - Psalm 90	80 Years
Second Coming	2029 A.D.
- Tribulation Period	7 Years
First Fruits Rapture	2022 A.D.

If the length of the generation Jesus was referring to in His parable of the "fig tree" is 70 to 80 years long, then the Second Coming of Jesus would not take place until around the year 2019 or 2029 A.D., with the Rapture of First Fruit believers occurring seven years earlier in 2012 or 2022 A.D. These dates are given as possibilities, however, they appear to be rather remote. If the end-time events were to occur at these times, the prophecy in Hosea 6:2, would need to be converted back to Solar years in order for it to agree with the above times:

Israel rejected Jesus	29 A.D.
+ 2,000 Solar Years	2000 Years
Second Coming	2029 A.D.
- Tribulation Period	7 Years
First Fruits Rapture	2022 A.D.

This is included above, but should be taken as a rather remote possibility. As we saw in the previous chapter, God deals in 360 day years. Why would He convert to using 365 day years for this prophecy?

OTHER CONSIDERATIONS

On August 2, 1990 Saddam Hussein invaded the country of Kuwait. Most students of God's Word agree that the Middle East war we witnessed was indeed described by the prophets (see Isaiah 13 & 21 and Jeremiah 50 & 51).

Notice what Isaiah had to say about Babylon:

"An oracle concerning Babylon [Iraq]. . . . "

"They come from faraway lands, from the ends of the heaven — the Lord and the weapons of his wrath — to destroy the whole country.

"Wail, for the DAY OF THE LORD is near; it will come like destruction from the Almighty" (Isaiah 13:1, 5-6).

Isaiah was telling those who witness them coming from a faraway land to destroy Babylon: to WAIL, for the DAY OF THE LORD is near. The war in the Persian Gulf brought armies from as far away as possible. This war with Iraq was definitely a sign to the world that the Day of the Lord is NEAR. How near is it? Let's see what else Isaiah has to say about the war that the world witnessed in 1990 and 1991:

"For thus hath the Lord said unto me, Within a year, according to the YEARS OF AN HIRELING, and all the glory of Kedar [Jordan] shall fail" (Isaiah 21:16, KJ).

The definition of the YEARS OF AN HIRELING is given to us in Isaiah 16:14, KJ:

". . . Within *three years*, as the *YEARS OF AN HIRELING*."

Isaiah is saying that the *years of an hireling* are equal to *three years*. In Isaiah 21:16, he is telling us that within three years all of Jordan will fail. Within 3 years of what? Let's look at the context in Isaiah 21:14-15:

"The inhabitants of the land of Tema brought water to him that was thirsty, they prevented with their bread him that FLED. For they FLED FROM THE SWORDS, from the drawn sword, and from the bent bow, and from the grievousness of war."

Isaiah places this three year time span from the time that they fled into Jordan from the threat of war. In 1990 and 1991, hundreds of thousands of refugees fled into Jordan for food, water and shelter from the coming war. This very well could be the situation the prophet Isaiah was referring to. If it is, he says that within 3 years, Jordan will fail.

In other words, three years from 1990-91 is 1993-94. If this interpretation is correct, another war will take place in the Middle East in 1993-94, and Jordan will fail at that time. The main point that needs to be remembered, however, is that the prophets were warning that the Day of the Lord is *NEAR!*

The above interpretation is brought out to show that there is other evidence that needs to be considered. Remember that now we look through the glass darkly. Once a particular prophecy is fulfilled, it is much easier to locate the Scripture involved. It is much more difficult to interpret a Scripture before it happens.

LOOKING FOR THAT BLESSED HOPE

From all of the clues and evidence we have seen, the Second Coming of Jesus Christ **could** be in 2000 A.D. This would mean that the most likely time for the Rapture of First Fruit believers would be in 1993.

While we cannot be dogmatic about this time, the First Fruit believer will hope that it is the correct interpretation of the Scripture. If 1993, is not the correct year, the Bride of Christ will continue LOOKING for her Bridegroom with the assurance that He is indeed returning for her and His return is that much closer. She will continue LOOKING FOR THAT BLESSED HOPE (Titus 2:13), knowing that He will remove His First Fruits prior to when the Day of the Lord begins.

We need to remember that Christ's First Coming was missed because of the attitude of the people. Let's not miss the timing of His Second Coming and Rapture for failure to discern the signs of the time and the signs given in the Word of God. The point needs to be understood that the *__end is near__* and the Bride of Christ should be aware of the time and *__looking__* for her Bridegroom.

CHAPTER 10

As It Was in the Days of Noah

In the previous chapter, we saw evidence that the Rapture of First Fruit believers **COULD** occur in 1993. We also saw that it could be in 1996, or even possibly as late as 2012 or 2022 A.D., although these latter dates are not considered as likely.

We now see through a glass darkly, but know that it is very near. As we approach that glorious Day, the wise will understand more; and perhaps, will even know the exact day shortly before it finally arrives.

EXAMPLE OF NOAH

In the story of Noah, we find that God told him the exact day of his deliverance, 7 days in advance:

"Seven days from now I will send rain on the earth for forty days and forty nights, and I will wipe from the face of the earth every living creature I have made" (Genesis 7:4).

Perhaps God will do the same for those living in these end-times. Remember, Jesus told us:

"As it was in the days of Noah, so it will be at the coming of the Son of Man" (Matthew 24:27).

In the Greek this reads: just as or exactly like it was in the days of Noah. Among other things, this could indicate that God will let His First Fruit believers know 7 days in advance of the time He plans to Rapture them to His throne. Remember from the first chapter of this book, the wise and faithful followers of Jesus are to know the time of their deliverance.

POSSIBLE TIMES

Since Jesus said His coming would be exactly like it was in the days of Noah, there are several possibilities as to what this may actually mean.

17th Day of Second Month

In the story of Noah, God recorded the exact day that Noah was delivered:

> "In the six hundredth year of Noah's life, in the SECOND MONTH, the SEVENTEENTH DAY of the month, the same day were all the fountains of the great deep broken up, and the windows of heaven were opened" (Genesis 7:11).

Could it be that Jesus was telling us, in the story of Noah, the exact day the First Fruit believers will be delivered? If so, the 17th day of the second month could be the time for the Rapture.

The Appendix lists the 17th day of the second month of Cheshvan over the next several years. It is very possible that the Rapture of First Fruit believers might occur on the anniversary of Noah's flood.

One thing these dates do not take into consideration, however, is that some contend that the correct way to reckon the time of the flood is from the fall equinox. In a book called: *THE LONG DAY OF JOSHUA*, the authors contend that the flood occurred on November 7, or 47 days (30 + 17) after the fall equinox in that year which was on September 21. If this is the correct method-ology to use, then the Rapture could be on this date.

GOG-MAGOG WAR

Many believe that the seven year Tribulation period may begin with the war outlined in Ezekiel 38 & 39, known as the Gog-Magog war. It is possible that Jesus was telling us that He will deliver us at the same time that this war takes place. This would be parallel with the fact that the flood came the same day Noah entered into the ark (see Genesis 7:11-12).

The Word of God seems to indicate when this great battle will occur. Notice the striking similarities between what the prophet Haggai and Ezekiel recorded:

> "This is what the Lord Almighty says: 'In a little while I will ONCE MORE SHAKE THE HEAVENS AND THE EARTH, THE SEA AND THE DRY LAND. I WILL SHAKE THE NATIONS. . . .' "

> "From this day on, from this TWENTY-FOURTH day of the NINTH month, give careful thought to the day when the foundation of the Lord's temple was laid. Give careful thought. . . . FROM THIS DAY ON I WILL BLESS YOU (ISRAEL). The word of the Lord came to Haggai a second time on the TWENTY-FOURTH day of the month. . . . I WILL SHAKE THE HEAVENS AND THE EARTH. I will overturn royal thrones and shatter the power of the foreign kingdoms. I will over-throw CHARIOTS and their drivers; HORSES and their riders will fall, EACH BY THE SWORD OF HIS BROTHER" (Haggai 2:6-7 & 2:18-22).

Now notice the resemblance to what the prophet Ezekiel had to say:

"You will come from your place in the far north, you and MANY NATIONS with you, all of them riding on HORSES, a great horde, a mighty army. THE MOUNTAINS WILL BE OVERTURNED, the CLIFFS WILL CRUMBLE and EVERY WALL WILL FALL TO THE GROUND. I will summon a SWORD against Gog on all my mountains, declares the Sovereign Lord. EVERY MAN'S SWORD WILL BE AGAINST HIS BROTHER. From that DAY FORWARD the house of Israel will know that I am their God" (Ezekiel 38:15, 20, 21, 22).

The close similarity of the wording these two prophets used could indicate they are talking about the same event. If this is so, the Gog-Magog war could occur on the 24th day of the 9th month. This would be on God's sacred calendar, or the month of Kislev. This could be the time for this war to occur and also the time that God delivers His First Fruits as an analogy to the Flood.

The Appendix also lists the 24th day of Kislev over the next several years. It is very possible that the Rapture of First Fruit believers might occur on this day.

RAPTURE OF ENOCH

A final possibility found in the story of Noah may be from Enoch — Noah's great grandfather. The Rapture of Enoch is found in Genesis 5:24:

"Enoch walked with God; then he was no more, because God took him away."

Enoch was the first person to ever be Raptured from the earth. Because Enoch walked with God, God removed him from the earth prior to when the wrath of the Flood arrived. While the Word of God does not indicate when this event occurred, there is a book entitled: *THE SECRETS OF ENOCH* which records that Enoch was Raptured on his birthday, the sixth of Sivan. The sixth of Sivan just happens to be the Feast of Pentecost. Enoch was born and also Raptured on Pentecost!

Another name for Pentecost is the Feast of Weeks or the Feast of Harvest. Notice that there are three annual festivals:

> "Three times a year you are to celebrate a festival to me. Celebrate the Feast of Unleavened Bread...in the month of Abib, for in that month you came out of Egypt. . . . "

> "Celebrate the Feast of Harvest with the **FIRST FRUITS** of the crops you sow in your field.

> "Celebrate the Feast of Ingathering at the end of the year when you gather in your crops from the field" (Exodus 23:14-16).

The second of the annual festivals was known as the Feast of Harvest or the Feast of Weeks. This was also described in Exodus 34:22:

> "Celebrate the Feast of Weeks with the **FIRSTFRUITS** of the wheat harvest. . . . "

The Feast of Weeks was the harvest festival celebrated with the FIRSTFRUITS of the wheat harvest. Both John the Baptist and Jesus referred to the believer as the wheat (see Matthew 3:12 and 13:30). The Feast of Weeks or Pentecost is the <u>time of celebration</u> for the FIRSTFRUITS of this wheat crop.

Pentecost is actually called the day of FIRST FRUITS:

> "On the *day of FIRSTFRUITS*, when you present to the Lord an offering of new grain during the Feast of Weeks . . . " (Numbers 28:26).

The day of *FIRSTFRUITS* is **Pentecost**. Enoch was Raptured on Pentecost as a type picture of the FIRST FRUIT believer. Because Enoch pleased God by walking with Him, God Raptured Enoch as a type picture on the day of Firstfruits or Pentecost.

Based upon this beautiful similitude, the Feast of Pentecost could very well be the time for God to Rapture His First Fruit believers from the earth. It is the day of Firstfruits and a Feast of Harvest. For those First Fruit believers walking with God, the Rapture could take them to be with God on this same day, the anniversary of the Rapture of Enoch, the day of FIRST FRUITS.

In the Appendix the reader will find a listing of the dates Pentecost falls on over the next several years. Of all the possible times that have been mentioned in this chapter, this Feast day appears to be the most likely time for the Rapture of First Fruit Believers. It meets the requirement of being "as in the days of Noah" since Enoch was born and Raptured on this day, and it is the actual day of **FIRST FRUITS** in celebration of the harvest of the firstfruits wheat crop. God will harvest His First Fruit believers prior to the general harvest at the Feast of Ingathering which will take place at the end of the Tribulation.

OTHER LESSONS

Other than the lessons that we have learned concerning the possible time of the Rapture, the Lord's words concerning Noah have other meanings that are equally interesting. Let's see what else we can learn from the days of Noah.

VIOLENCE & WICKEDNESS

One of the major signs that tells us that the coming of the Lord is drawing near is the tremendous amount of violence and wickedness that is witnessed around the world. Jesus said exactly like it was in the days of Noah, so will it be at the time He is about to return. Notice what the Word of God says it was like at the time of Noah:

"The Lord saw how great man's wickedness on the earth had become, and that every inclination of the thoughts of his heart was only evil all the time.

"Now the earth was corrupt in God's sight and was full of violence. God saw how corrupt the earth had become, for all the people on earth had corrupted their ways. So God said to Noah, 'I am going to put an end to all people, for the earth is filled with violence because of them. I am surely going to destroy both them and the earth' " (Genesis 6:5, 11, 12 & 13).

Because of the violence and wickedness in Noah's day, God destroyed the people with the Flood. Today, the news is filled with stories of violence and wickedness. America rates as the worst in the world in terms of violence. The world has become exactly like it was at the time of Noah, and as a result, God is getting ready to unleash the horrors of the Tribulation upon mankind.

FEW TAKEN

Also notice from the story of Noah, that only a few were taken. Enoch was taken from the Earth before the Flood came and Noah and his family were saved on the very day that the Flood arrived. Only a total of eight people were brought into the safety of the Ark. This represents only a very small percentage of the people on the earth at that time, because Genesis 6:1, indicates that the population was expanding.

Jesus said His coming would be exactly like it was in Noah's day. Based upon this account of Noah, very few people will be delivered prior to when the Tribulation begins. The First Fruit believers represent a very small percentage of today's population: a parallel with the size of Noah's family in relationship to the people of that time. Remember that the Lord said, "For many are called, but few are chosen" (Matthew 22:14).

NOAH KNEW DATE — 7 DAY WARNING

We need to remember that God told Noah the exact date when the flood would arrive (see Genesis 7:4 & 11). God gave Noah a 7 day warning that the Flood was coming. Since Jesus said that His coming would be exactly like it was in the days of Noah, the First Fruit believers may receive a 7 day warning. We cannot be certain that this is a correct interpretation of our Lord's meaning, but it is highly possible.

ENOCH & NOAH WALKED WITH GOD

The Word of God indicates that both Enoch and Noah walked with God (see Genesis 5:24 & 6:9). Because these righteous men walked with God, they were preserved from harm. Enoch was removed from the earth via Rapture, while Noah was protected in the Ark. Enoch pleased God (Hebrews 11:5) and Noah was a righteous and blameless man (Genesis 6:9). Because of these characteristics, God saved these men from the wrath of the Flood.

As God saved these Godly men, He will also keep the righteous, blameless believer from the coming Tribulation. Those who are walking with God and pleasing Him by the way they are living, will be taken to the throne of God to protect them from the trials to come.

FAITH REQUIRED

One final lesson we will learn from Enoch and Noah is the necessity of faith.

Hebrews 11:5 says, "By FAITH Enoch was taken from this life, so that he did not experience death [ie, Raptured]." Notice that it took FAITH to be Raptured. Many people do not believe in the Rapture, and many Christians do not even have the faith that is required in order to be Raptured. Faith requires belief followed by action. Faith believes that the time of the Rapture is rapidly drawing near. Faith motivates the believer to get ready, and to tell others to prepare. From Enoch, we can learn that FAITH is a prerequisite in order to be Raptured.

Hebrews 11:7 says, "By faith Noah, when warned about things not yet seen, in holy fear built an ark to save his family. . . . " It took faith to prepare for the coming Flood. Because Noah believed God's words to him, he was obedient and took action to get ready. In a similar manner today, the people with faith will take the necessary actions to prepare themselves. They will believe God's Word and do what it says. By faith, they will make themselves ready to meet Him. As a Bride preparing for her wedding, the people of faith will be getting ready to meet their Bridegroom when He calls.

CHAPTER 11

Final Preparations

We have seen that a potentially devastating SPIRITUAL EARTHQUAKE is about to hit! Once it arrives, there will be no turning back. People will not be given another chance. God will remove the First Fruit believers who are prepared and ready to meet Him. Those found walking with Him and worthy in His sight will have the glorious privilege of being with Him.

All others will be faced with the horrors of the Tribulation. After the Rapture of First Fruit believers takes place, the Antichrist will be revealed (II Thessalonians 2:7-8), and he will perform all kinds of counterfeit miracles with great signs and wonders. He will appear to be Christ, but he will be a counterfeit.

Many PROFESSING or NOMINAL Christians will follow him. Notice why:

> "The coming of the lawless one will be in accordance with the work of Satan displayed in all kinds of counterfeit miracles, signs and wonders, and in every sort of evil that deceives those who are perishing. They perish because THEY REFUSED TO LOVE THE TRUTH AND BE SAVED.

> "For this reason God sends them a POWERFUL DELUSION so that they will BELIEVE the LIE and so that all will be condemned who have not believed the

truth but have delighted in wickedness" (II Thessalonians 2:9-12).

Those who call themselves Christians, but do not truly LOVE THE TRUTH will be sent a very strong delusion from God! Because they are not really saved, they will not be given another chance. They will condemn themselves by believing the delusion God sends them.

CHURCH SHAKEN

God will truly shake the Church after His First Fruit believers are taken from this planet. As we have seen, the professing or nominal Christian will follow the lie. They lose their chance of ever seeing Heaven.

However, there will be a great multitude of real Christians remaining. These will be truly born-again believers who failed to prepare to meet the Bridegroom. They will recognize the Antichrist for who he really is, and they will not believe the lie.

After the shattering EARTHQUAKE, the greatest AFTER-SHOCKS to follow will be when these very Christians realize they were misled. They were not taken in the Rapture because their Pastors and Teachers (who should have known) failed in their duties as Watchmen and taught false doctrine. That is why Jesus urged His disciples not be be led astray by *ANY* man (Matthew 24:4).

Their anger, remorse and regret will need to be put behind them quickly. The Church will need to come together to help and encourage one another. They will now be faced with the reality that martyrdom will probably be required of them. Those days will be some of the most perilous times one could imagine. If they are not killed by war first, they will become those described in Revelation 12:11:

"They overcame him by the blood of the Lamb and

by the word of their testimony; they did not love their lives so much as to shrink from death."

People will be required to receive a mark on their right hand or forehead. The only other alternative will be death. The true Christian will stand up for Jesus and refuse to receive the mark. They will be killed, but they will be assured of going to be with the Lord. If they receive the mark, they seal their fate in hell:

> "If anyone worships the beast and his image and receives his mark on the forehead or on the hand, he, too, will drink of the wine of God's fury, which has been poured full strength into the cup of his wrath. He will be tormented with burning sulfur in the presence of the holy angels and of the Lamb" (Revelation 14:9-10).

TIME TO PREPARE

If you are reading this book prior to when the Rapture takes place, you still have time to prepare to take part in it. You are probably in one of the following categories:

1) Unrighteous and lost.

2) Professing or Nominal Christian.

3) Born-again with defiled garments.

4) First Fruit prepared believer.

UNRIGHTEOUS & LOST

If you do not know Jesus Christ as your Lord and Savior, and you are reading this book, you need to come to a personal relationship with Him now. Jesus came and died for your sins, that you might not have to pay the penalty. He not only died for your sins, but He also rose from the dead. He conquered death so that you might live. You need to ask Jesus to come into your heart as your own personal Savior and Lord. Why not pray a prayer like the one below right now:

> *"Dear God in Heaven, I don't fully understand everything about this, but I know that I am a sinner and that I need a Savior. Thank you for sending your Son, Jesus to die for my sins and pay the penalty. I humbly ask Jesus to come into my heart and life to be my personal Lord and Savior. Help me to live the remainder of my life for you, being led by your Holy Spirit. Please count me worthy to escape all that is about to happen on this earth. In the precious name of Jesus Christ, I pray. Amen."*

If you sincerely prayed this prayer, praise the Lord! He has saved your soul, and you are now Born-again. You will want to make sure that you follow through with the above prayer by reading His Word and praying to Him every day. Find a church where the Word of God is preached, and be sure to tell others about your new faith in Jesus Christ and the fact that He is coming back again very soon!

PROFESSING OR NOMINAL CHRISTIAN

If you profess Jesus Christ, are you living the way Christ tells you to? Are you living as Christ did?

> "Someone may say, 'I am a Christian; I am on my way to heaven; I belong to Christ.' But if he doesn't <u>do</u> what Christ tells him to, <u>he is a liar</u>. But those who do what Christ tells them to will learn to love God more and more. That is the way to know whether or not you are a Christian. Anyone who says he is a Christian should live as Christ did" (I John 2:4-5, LB).

There are many people who profess to be born-again believers. Only Christ knows their hearts and whether or not they truly love Him. If upon examining your heart, in all honesty, you realize you are not truly a Christian, humbly repent right now. Pray the same prayer given above with true sincerity. Completely yield your life to Him and ask Him to be your Master and Savior. God does love you, and He wants to be your everything!

BORN-AGAIN WITH DEFILED GARMENTS

The book of Revelation indicates that there will be a great multitude of believers who will be required to become martyrs (please see Revelation 7:9-17). This portion of the Word of God tells us that there will be many born-again believers who will enter the horror of the Tribulation period. They were Christians before it began because they had their robes. The reason they were required to go into the Tribulation period is shown in verse 14:

"They have washed their robes and made them white in the blood of the Lamb."

These born-again believers had soiled their garments and needed to wash them to make them white again. They were not as careful as the few found in the church of Sardis:

"Thou hast a few names even in Sardis which have not defiled their garments; and they shall walk with me in white: for they are worthy" (Revelation 3:4, KJ).

These few in Sardis had kept their garments white and were found worthy. These are the First Fruit believers that made the necessary preparations by walking with the Lord in obedience to His Word. They are the overcomers who pleased God and were found looking for Him when the Rapture took place.

For those readers who are born-again with defiled garments, let's look at the preparations that are required in order to be found worthy; and some attributes of First Fruit believers.

KEEP GOD'S WORD

Revelation 3:10 reminds us:

> "Because thou hast **kept the word** of my patience, I also will keep thee from the hour of temptation, which shall come upon all the world, to try them that dwell upon the earth."

The believer who is obedient to God's Word is given the wonderful promise of escaping the Tribulation period.

WALK IN LIGHT

I John 1:7 instructs us:

> "But if we **walk in the light**, as he is in the light, we have fellowship with one another, and the blood of Jesus, his Son, purifies us from all sin."

The believer needs to walk in the light as opposed to walking in darkness. This means that the believer should separate themselves from any sin. If there is *any sin* in the life of the believer, they should **REPENT** (turn away from it) and ask for forgiveness from the Lord:

"If we confess our sins, he is faithful and just and will forgive us our sins and purify us from all unrighteousness" (I John 1:9).

PLEASE GOD

As we have seen, the First Fruit believers are proteges of Enoch. Remember what was said of him in Hebrews 11:5:

> "...For before he was taken [Raptured], he was commended as one who **PLEASED GOD**."

The believer will want to please the Lord by the life that they live. The motives of the First Fruit believer will always be to please God.

WITNESS

One other big lesson that can be learned from Enoch, is that the believer should be actively witnessing to others that Jesus is getting ready to return. Notice what is said of Enoch in Jude 14:

"And Enoch also, the seventh from Adam, prophesied of these, saying, BEHOLD, THE LORD COMETH with ten thousands of his saints."

Telling others to come to the Lord and the fact that **JESUS IS COMING** very soon is a very important part in the life of the believer. The Word of God says very little about Enoch. What it does say should be listened to very carefully. Telling others the Lord is coming is VERY important.

PERSEVERE

The believer needs to remember the example of Paul who always "pressed toward the mark for the prize of the high calling." Paul was diligent and he persevered until the end of his life. The believer worthy of this prize will heed the Lord's words in Luke 9:62:

"Jesus replied, 'No one who puts his hand to the plow and looks back is fit for service in the kingdom of God.' "

By not looking back the Lord means living their lives the way they used to live before they were saved. Many born-again believers have returned to living their lives the way they were before salvation. The Church has gotten SO Lukewarm, that there is very little difference between the world and the Church.

The believer will want to remember the story of Lot's wife. She had grown too attached to the place she was leaving. She didn't really want to leave it. She looked back, and was destroyed. The believer should not grow too attached to this world. Their real home is in heaven, but too many believers are looking back. They need to REPENT and stop being friends with this world. Remember Lot's wife and remember the words of James:

"Anyone who chooses to be a friend of the world becomes an enemy of God" (James 4:4).

BE HUMBLE

The believer will want to remember that true humility is something to be highly valued:

"Blessed are the poor in spirit: for theirs is the kingdom of heaven" (Matthew 5:3, KJ).

The humble believer is given the wonderful assurance by our Lord, that their inheritance is the Kingdom.

BE HOLY

Holiness is a major ingredient that is missing from the Church today. The believer should make sure they are living a holy life:

"*MAKE EVERY EFFORT* to live in peace with all men and TO BE **HOLY**; without holiness no one will see the Lord" (Hebrews 12:14).

It is the responsibility of every believer to heed these words. For those believers who have not been living holy lives, they should REPENT and begin leading holy lives from here on, until the Lord returns.

BE BLAMELESS

In line with holiness, the believer needs to make every effort to be blameless and pure:

"So then, dear friends, since you are looking forward to this, *MAKE EVERY EFFORT* to be found **SPOT-LESS, BLAMELESS** and at **PEACE** with him" (II Peter 3:14).

While the believer will not reach spotless perfection until the Lord returns, the Born-again believer should be making every effort to be blameless and pure. It is the attitude and the motive of the heart that will determine if a person is making the effort required to have them found blameless. God knows those who are trying to please Him by looking into their heart.

BE WATCHFUL

The Word of God is filled with examples that teach the believer to be looking for and eagerly expecting the return of the Lord. A few of these are outlined below:

" . . . You ought to live holy and godly lives as you LOOK FORWARD to the day of God. . . . So then, dear friends, since you are LOOKING FORWARD to this" (II Peter 3:11 & 14).

"But our citizenship is in heaven. And we EA-GERLY AWAIT a Savior from there, the Lord Jesus Christ . . . " (Philippians 3:20).

"LOOKING FOR that Blessed Hope" (Titus 2:13).

"Be always on the WATCH . . . " (Luke 21:36).

" . . . and unto them that LOOK FOR HIM shall he appear the second time . . . " (Hebrews 9:28).

The above is only a very small sample of some of the Scriptures telling the believer to be alert and watching for the Lord to return. The Lord commanded the believer to always be on the watch. He is returning for those believers who are eagerly waiting and looking for Him.

BE PRAYERFUL

Finally, the believer will realize that being found worthy to be included as part of the First Fruit group rests in the hands of the Lord. Because of this, Jesus instructed His humble followers to pray:

> "Watch ye therefore, and ***PRAY ALWAYS***, that ye may be ***accounted worthy to escape*** all these things that shall come to pass, and to stand before the Son of man" (Luke 21:36, KJ).

The believer realizes that being found worthy to escape the Tribulation, depends upon the grace and mercy of the Lord. The believer will make every effort to be obedient to Him, and will humbly pray to be considered worthy.

FINAL PREPARATIONS

Until the cataclysmic SPIRITUAL EARTHQUAKE occurs, the reader can be included in the select group of First Fruit believers.

Remember the story of the thief dying on the cross next to Jesus:

> "And he said unto Jesus, LORD, remember me when thou comest into thy kingdom. And Jesus said unto him, Verily I say unto thee, Today shalt thou be with me in paradise" (Luke 23:42-43, KJ).

This story is a beautiful example of the love and mercy of our Lord. Right up until the very time that this thief was about to die, this thief was lost. Then, he realized who Jesus was. He humbly asked Jesus to remember him. He called Him Lord. He was saved at the very last moment, and given the assurance of being with Jesus.

In a similar manner, the person reading this book has the chance to humbly turn to Jesus and ask Him to count him worthy of escaping the horrible times ahead. Why not pray the following prayer right now:

> *"Dear God in Heaven, please help me to live my life in such a way that it is pleasing to you. Please consider me worthy to escape the time that is coming to test this world. In the name of Jesus, my Lord, I pray. Amen."*

If you prayed the above prayer with a humble heart, you have made the most essential preparations to meet Him. Now, CONTINUE living for Him in holiness and looking for Him until He returns (I John 2:28).

Index to Questions & Answers

Index to Questions & Answers (Continued)

Index to Questions & Anwers (Continued)

If the reader has any more questions please call or write:

Jim Harman
P.O. Box 941612
Maitland, FL 32794
(407) 834-4106

QUESTION:

A. Revelation 14, shows only 144,000 First Fruit believers. How many people are included in the Rapture of First Fruit believers?

ANSWER:

A literal interpretation of the Greek in Revelation 14:1, would mean 144,000. The question then becomes: should this passage be taken literally, or should it be considered symbolic?

The book of Revelation is filled with symbolism. It is **VERY** possible that this number of 144,000 is meant as a symbolic representation to demonstrate that the total number of First Fruit believers is limited. In this case, it would mean that there are **many more** than this number, but that it is a select group.

It is hoped this interpretation is correct and the number of First Fruit believers are many more than this number of only 144,000.

QUESTION:

B. Jude 14, shows only 10,000 saints returning with Jesus. Is that all who will be Raptured?

ANSWER:

First, let's review what Jude 14 says:

"And Enoch also, the seventh from Adam prophesied of these, saying, Behold the Lord cometh with ten thousands of his saints" (Jude 14, KJ).

The above quote was taken from the King James version. The New International version says, *" . . . with thousands upon thousands of his holy ones. "* Let's look at the Interlinear Bible which is a more literal translation of the original Greek:

"And Enoch, the seventh from Adam, also prophesied to these men, saying, Behold, the Lord came with *myriads* of His saints."

The Greek uses the word: murias (#3611) which means: ten thousand or a myriad number or indefinite number.

This same word (#3611) is used in Acts 19:19, and Revelation 9:16. In both of these cases, it means a literal 10,000.

However, in Hebrews 12:22, this same word is used to mean "myriads" or an indefinite number.

After studying all of the various places the word murias is used, it is determined that we cannot be 100% certain whether Enoch saw 10,000 Saints or an indefinite number of Saints returning with the Lord. It could be only 10,000, but it also could be an indefinite number.

We hope and pray that it is indeed a myriad of Saints returning with the Lord and not just 10,000.

May the Lord reach myriads of Saints with the message of this book to help sway this issue in favor of there being an untold great number of Saints returning with Him.

QUESTION:

C. What is the "falling away" in II Thessalonians 2:3?

ANSWER:

II Thessalonians 2:3, KJ says:

"Let no man deceive you by any means: for that day [Day of the Lord] shall not come, except there come a falling away first, and that man of sin be revealed, the son of perdition [Anti-christ]."

This is saying that the falling away and the revelation of the

Anti-christ will occur before the Day of the Lord begins.

However, before the Anti-christ is revealed, remember that "He" must be taken out of the way. From chapter 5, we saw that this "He" is the MALE CHILD of Revelation 12:5, or the Overcoming First Fruit believers. Only after they are Raptured, may the Anti-christ be revealed (See II Thessalonians 2:6-8.)

But what about the "falling away," what is Paul referring to? The Greek word that is used is: apostasia (#646). This means defection, falling away, or to forsake. From this, many have felt Paul was referring to a falling away from the faith. This is also talked about in I Timothy 4:1. If this falling away from the faith is what Paul meant, it appears that it has begun and is continuing. Sound doctrine is no longer upheld by many and various "doctrines of devils" have permeated the Church.

While the above interpretation may be right, there is another possibility. In seven of the first English translations before the King James Version the word apostasia is translated as "departynge." This would mean that Paul was saying that the departure must occur first. Or that the Rapture must happen before the Day of the Lord begins. This is in line with what has been shown in this book, and probably is a better exegesis of this passage.

QUESTION:

D. In Revelation 12, who is the "Woman"? and the "rest of her offspring" (v.17)?

ANSWER:

The "Woman" of Revelation 12:1, appears to be Israel (please see Genesis 37:9-10). She is the one responsible for the birth of the Church. Through Israel, Christ was born, and Christ is the head of the Church. (Also read Romans 9:4-5 and Colossians 1:18.)

In chapter 5, we saw that the MALE CHILD the woman gave birth to is the overcoming First Fruit believer. For further proof of this, notice who "the rest of her offspring" are:

"And the dragon was wroth with the woman, and went to make war with the REMNANT of HER SEED, which keep the commandments of God, and HAVE the TESTIMONY of Jesus Christ" (Revelation 12:17, KJ).

In this story, Satan goes after Israel, but is unable to harm her (see verse 14). He then goes after the woman's offspring. In verse 17, we see that her offspring are the remnant of Christians remaining. This ties the "offspring" with the MALE CHILD. They were both born from the same mother: the "woman" described earlier. The "offspring" are pictured as believers which means that they could not be a Jewish remnant. They are Christians being pursued by the Anti-christ during the Tribulation. They were directly related to the MALE CHILD, having the same mother: the "woman."

The above explanation further enhances the argument that the MALE CHILD is the First Fruit believer. He is pictured as one of the offsprings from the "woman" which means he is directly related to the "other offspring." The First Fruit believers are directly related to the Christians who will enter the Tribulation to be pursued by the Anti-christ.

QUESTION:

E. What is the "Mystery of God" described in Revelation 10:7?

ANSWER:

Revelation 10:7, says:

"But in the days when the **seventh** angel is about to SOUND his TRUMPET, the *MYSTERY of God* will be accomplished, just as he announced to his servants the prophets."

This occurs when the seventh trumpet or the "last trumpet" is about to sound. In context with Revelation 11:15-19, this is at the very end of the Tribulation.

Notice that it says the "mystery of God" is accomplished as told to God's servants. This mystery was hidden, but then revealed:

" . . . according to the dispensation of God which is given to me for you, to fulfill the word of God; Even the MYSTERY which hath been hid from ages and from generations but now is made manifest to his saints.

"To whom God would make known what is the riches of the glory of this MYSTERY among the Gentiles; which is Christ in you, the hope of glory" (Colossians 1:25-27, KJ).

This MYSTERY is the mystery of God working in the Gentiles, reconciling men to Himself. Paul also spoke of it in Ephesians 3:3-6:

" . . . the MYSTERY made known to me by revelation . . . you will be able to understand my insight into the MYSTERY of Christ, which was not made known to men in other generations as it has now been revealed by the Spirit of God's holy apostles and prophets.

"This MYSTERY is that through the gospel the Gentiles are heirs together with Israel, members together of one body, and sharers together in the promise of Christ Jesus."

This MYSTERY is clearly the mystery of God working in history, bringing both Jews and Gentiles together in Christ.

Revelation 10 says when the seventh trumpet sounds, this mystery will be finished. This final dispensation of God will be over, and the Millennium will begin.

One other reference that Paul made to this MYSTERY is found in I Corinthians 15:51-52:

> "Behold, I show you a MYSTERY; We shall not all sleep, but we shall all be changed, in a moment, in the twinkling of eye, at the LAST TRUMP: for the TRUMPET shall SOUND, and the dead shall be raised incorruptible, and we shall be changed."

This traditional pre-tribulation verse ties in perfectly with Revelation 10:7. Both indicate the last trumpet will sound and both speak of the MYSTERY of God.

From the foregoing, the MYSTERY of God will be accomplished when the Tribulation period comes to an end at the sounding of the last trumpet. The MYSTERY of God bringing Jews and Gentiles together in Christ will be complete.

QUESTION:

F. Explain the difference between the Body of Christ and the Bride of Christ.

ANSWER:

The Body of Christ is made up of all truly born-again believers. It is mentioned in several places in the Word of God:

> "Now you [Christian] are the body of Christ, and each one of you is a part of it" (I Corinthians 12:27).

> " . . . so in Christ we who are many form one body, and each member belongs to all the others" (Romans 12:5).

Now, let's compare this description of the Body of Christ

with the Bride of Christ:

> "Let us rejoice and be glad and give him glory! For
> the wedding of the Lamb has come, and His *BRIDE has
> MADE HERSELF READY*" (Revelation 19:6-7).

The distinguishing characteristic of the Bride, is that she took
action once she was saved and *made herself ready*. As a result,
she is clothed in fine linen:

> "Fine linen, bright and clean, was given her to wear.
> Fine linen stands for the righteous ACTS of the saints"
> (Revelation 19:8).

The righteous ACTS of the saints are what set the Bride
apart.

There are two ways that the Christian can receive the "fine
linen, bright and clean." They can live their lives in such a way
that their good works are duly rewarded, at the Judgement Seat
of Christ, or they can "wash their robes and make them white in
the blood of the Lamb" (Revelation 7:14).

The Christian can either prepare before the Tribulation
begins through their righteous acts, or they can stand up for Jesus
through martyrdom. Either way, they will receive the proper
dress for their wedding.

But notice that some Christians will not be given these
wedding garments. They will not be part of the Bride, and will
miss the 1,000 year Millennium Kingdom (Matthew 22):

> "But when the king came in to see the guests, he
> noticed a man there who was not wearing wedding
> clothes. 'Friend,' he asked, 'How did you get in here
> without wedding clothes?' The man was speechless.
> Then the king told the attendants, 'Tie him hand and foot,
> and throw him outside, into the darkness, where

there will be weeping and gnashing of teeth.' For many
are invited, but few are chosen."

The above parable teaches us that some will be kept from the
wedding and the 1,000 year reign with Christ. The man without
the proper wedding garments, represents those born-again believers who did not make the necessary preparations as described
in the last chapter of this book. They will miss the Rapture and
they will miss the Millennial Kingdom. They are not part of the
Bride, but they are part of the Body of Christ. They will be joined
with the rest of the Body at the end of the Millennium.

Some might argue, how can you separate the Body of Christ
like that? Well, isn't the Body of Christ separated now? Hasn't
the Body of Christ been separated for almost 1,960 years? What
is an additional 1,000 years by God's timetable? Remember
1,000 years is only a day to God.

QUESTION:

G. When do the martyred saints in Revelation 7 get resurrected?

ANSWER:

The resurrection of the martyred saints is recorded in Revelation 20:4-5:

"I saw **thrones** on which **were seated** those who had
been given authority to judge. **And** I saw the **SOULS** of
those who had been beheaded because of their testimony
for Jesus and because of the word of God. They had not
worshiped the beast or his image and had not received his
mark on their foreheads or their hands. **THEY CAME
TO LIFE** and reigned with Christ a thousand years.
. . . This is the first resurrection. . . . "

Notice that at first, John only saw the First Fruit believers seated on their thrones along with the SOULS of the martyred saints. This tells us that the First Fruit believers had <u>previously</u> risen. <u>Then</u> John saw the martyred saints come to life. This is called the first resurrection. This resurrection of the martyred saints occurs at the end of man's 6,000 years and right before the 1,000 year Kingdom reign.

QUESTION:

H. How can you say Christians will enter the Tribulation period when I Thessalonians 5:9 says they are not appointed to suffer wrath?

ANSWER:

I Thessalonians 5:9, KJ says:

"For God hath not *appointed* us to wrath, but to obtain salvation by our Lord Jesus Christ."

The word for appointed (#5087) can mean: commit, conceive, make, ordain, purpose, put, set or sink.

The same word is also used in the following verses:

" . . . I have chosen you, and ordained [#5087] you, that you should go and bring forth fruit" (John 15:16).

" . . . hath made [#5087] you overseers to feed the church of God" (Acts 20:28).

God has ordained that the Christian should bring forth fruit. Is every Christian fruitful? The answer is no. While God has purposed ALL to be fruitful, not all will be.

In the same manner, God has purposed the overseers to feed the Church. Do all who have been called to feed, do so? Here again, the answer is no. Not all are feeding the Church as they have been called to do.

From these two examples, we can apply this to the "appointed" in I Thessalonians 5:9.

It is not God's *purpose* for Christians to have to suffer wrath. While He has not ordained that they SHOULD have to suffer wrath, the Word of God clearly indicates that some will:

" . . . These are they who have **come out of** the great tribulation . . . " (Revelation 7:14).

"Then the dragon was enraged at the woman and went off to make war against the **rest** of her **offspring** — **those** who obey God's commandments and hold to the testimony of Jesus" (Revelation 12:17).

"This calls for patient endurance on the part of the **saints** who obey God's commandments and remain faithful to Jesus" (Revelation 14:12).

God did not make it so Christians should have to suffer wrath. In His plan of things, He did not **"appoint"** them to have to suffer. While He has not purposed that Christians SHOULD suffer, this does not mean that ALL Christians will escape the wrath that is coming. The word Paul uses does not mean that every Christian will escape the wrath. Only those found "worthy" to escape, will escape.

QUESTION:

I.   What about the Mid-Tribulation theory of the Rapture? Please discuss it in light of the concept of a First Fruits Rapture.

ANSWER:

The Mid-Tribulation theory says that the Rapture takes place in the middle of the Tribulation. This is completely different from what Revelation 14 teaches. (See the fifth chapter of this book.) The First Fruit believers are taken to Heaven *__before__* the hour of Judgement arrives.

The Mid-Tribulationists and those adhering to the Pre-Wrath view are not truly LOOKING for the BLESSED HOPE, but are looking for the appearance of the Anti-christ. This is clearly in contradiction to Scripture (see Titus 1:9 and Titus 2:1-15). Remember that obedience to God's Word is what matters:

> "Because thou hast KEPT THE WORD of my patience, I also will keep thee from the hour of temptation" (Revelation 3:10, KJ).

Ironically, by adhering to these false teachings, it may prove to be self-fulfilling for their followers.

QUESTION:

J.   How can a person be assured of taking part in the Rapture?

ANSWER:

First of all, the individual needs to be 100% certain they are indeed born-again.

Being born-again means to have come to the cross of Jesus Christ in all humility and asking Him to come into their heart and life. By completely surrendering one's life and committing it to Him, the person dies to self and thus becomes "born-again."

Once a person is born-again, they will begin to show evidence of this experience. They will have a desire to read God's Word and pray to the Lord. In this new life as a Christian, the person will seek to be led by the Holy Spirit in obedience to God's Word. Additional evidence of **true** conversion will normally include:

> Baptism
> Witnessing
> Tithing
> Worshiping.

The Word of God indicates that only those who have KEPT GOD'S WORD and who have NOT DEFILED THEIR GARMENTS are counted worthy of escaping the Tribulation period. Some born-again believers are given the chance of escape because they heeded the Word of God and did what it says. They separated themselves from this world and pleased God by their righteous walk with Him as King.

To be assured of taking part in the Rapture of First Fruit believers, the person should continue living a sanctified life that will be pleasing to Him. They should make every effort to be found blameless in the Lord's eyes. Finally, they should:

> "WATCH ye therefore, and PRAY ALWAYS, that ye may be accounted worthy to escape all these things that shall come to pass, and to stand before the Son of man" (Luke 21:36, KJ).

QUESTION:

K. How can a Christian be excluded from the Kingdom? Aren't all Christians assured of going to Heaven?

ANSWER:

The distinction needs to be made between Heaven and the Kingdom. All truly born-again believers are assured of going to Heaven because their names are written in the Lamb's book of life:

> " . . . You have come to thousands upon thousands of angels in joyful assembly, to the church of the first-born, whose NAMES ARE WRITTEN IN HEAVEN" (Hebrews 12:22-23).

Only those whose names have not been written in the Lamb's book of life will go to hell:

"If anyone's name was not found written in the book of life, he was thrown into the lake of fire" (Revelation 20:15).

Entrance into the Kingdom is another matter. The Kingdom refers to the 1,000 year reign with Christ known as the Millennium. Not all born-again believers are assured of taking part in this Kingdom:

"Not everyone who says to me, 'Lord, Lord,' will enter the ***KINGDOM OF HEAVEN***, but only he who does the will of my Father who is in heaven" (Matthew 7:21).

These are our Lord's own words that not all Christians will enter the Kingdom, or the 1,000 year reign with Him. In addition to other parables referred to in Chapter 7, the Lord also taught this concept in Luke 20:35:

"But THOSE who are considered WORTHY of taking part in THAT AGE and in the resurrection from the dead. . . . "

Jesus said only those who are considered WORTHY will take part in THAT AGE or the Kingdom age, which begins at the first resurrection.

At the end of the Millennium, all Christians who missed the Kingdom reign, will be raised to life. Since their names are written in the book of life, they are assured of going to Heaven at that time.

While all Christians will not participate in the 1,000 year Kingdom reign, ALL true Christians will go to Heaven.

QUESTION:

L. Why hasn't the Church been taught about the partial Rapture and the concept of the Kingdom?

ANSWER:

Remember, Ecclesiastes 3:15 tells us everything that is, has been before:

"Whatever is has already been, and what will be has been before. . . . "

When Jesus observed the condition of the Church and its leaders, notice what He had to say (Matthew 23:13-14):

"Woe to you, teachers of the law and Pharisees, you hypocrites! You *shut* the *kingdom of heaven* in men's faces. You yourselves do not enter, nor will you let those enter who are trying to."

Nothing has really changed from the time of Jesus. The religious leaders at that time were not teaching what the people needed to know. They were really hypocrites keeping others from the correct path.

Today, the same thing is happening again. Teachings about a partial Rapture and the Kingdom are not being taught because it is the truth. The current day Pastors and Teachers are, once again, keeping the people from entering the Kingdom, by not "rightly dividing" the Word of truth.

Instead, much of the Church is guilty of allowing incorrect teachings to prevail. No longer is sound doctrine encouraged as it should be (Titus 1:9 & 2:1), but the Church has fulfilled yet another Scripture:

"For the time will come when men will not put up

with sound doctrine. Instead, to suit their own desires, they will gather around them a GREAT NUMBER of teachers to say what their ITCHY EARS want to hear" (II Timothy 4:3).

The religious leaders of today need to re-evaluate what is being taught. The Church members need to insist upon the return to sound doctrine.

QUESTION:

M. Is there other evidence the Middle East war will start-up again soon?

ANSWER:

Besides the fact that we know the Middle East is being armed for war, the Word of God also tells us that another war is about to take place. In addition to the Scripture verses discussed in Chapter 9, the prophet Jeremiah also indicated that the war is not over yet:

> "And lest your heart faint, and ye fear for the rumor that shall be heard in the land; a rumor shall both come one year, and after that in another year shall come a rumor, and violence in the land, ruler against ruler" (Jeremiah 51:46, KJ).

This indicates that a war will occur in one year, and that it will start-up again in another year. In a previous verse, the prophet gives us an indication as to the timing:

> "This is what the Lord Almighty, the God of Israel, says: 'The Daughter of Babylon is like a threshing floor *at the time it is trampled; the time to harvest her will soon*

come' " (Jeremiah 51:33).

The war we witnessed in Iraq (Babylon) is brought out in the first part of this verse as the time it was trampled. The United Nations, led by the great American armed forces certainly trampled Iraq. The prophet says that after Babylon is trampled, the time to harvest her will soon come.

We are not given the number of years, but Jeremiah indicates that it will not be long between the time Babylon is trampled and then harvested. This substantiates what was brought out in Chapter 9, where it was shown Isaiah taught there would be three years between the time of fighting.

The Middle East may erupt again soon. The point needs to be remembered that the Old Testament Prophets were predicting a time which was far into the future. The study of Prophecy should remind the believer the return of the Lord is near; and of their need to be ready.

Although there is a great deal of evidence that the Rapture *could* occur in 1993, we need to remember:

> "For now we SEE through a glass, DARKLY; but then face to face: now I KNOW IN PART; but then shall I know even as also I am known" (I Corinthians 13:12, KJ).

If the Rapture doesn't occur this year, one of the reasons may be the long-suffering and mercy of God:

> "The Lord is not slack concerning his promise as some men count slackness; but is long-suffering to us-ward, not willing that any should perish, but that all should come to repentance" (II Peter 3:9).

God is merciful, and He doesn't want anyone to perish. While it may appear that God is being slack in His return, His reason may be to give people more time to prepare.

If the Lord does not return this year, the believer should continue looking for Him until He returns.

The words from Matthew Henry's commentary are good advice for the wise:

> "Therefore every day and every hour we must be ready, and not off our watch any day in the year, or any hour in the day" (M.H. Volume 5, Page 372).

QUESTION:

N. How can there be a "Blessed Hope" if the Church has to go into the Tribulation period?

ANSWER:

The Blessed Hope is found in Titus 2:13(KJ):

> "Looking for that blessed hope, and the glorious appearing of the great God and our Savior Jesus Christ."

The Blessed Hope is the hope that Christ will take us to be with Him. We should be looking for that time and eagerly awaiting His call.

The problem arises, from the fact that the entire Church is not looking for the soon return of the Lord, and they do not have the Blessed Hope in their hearts.

The Blessed Hope is REAL, but it is only real to those who have "eyes to see and ears to hear." Only those who are obedient to the Word will have the Blessed Hope:

"Behold, I am coming soon! BLESSED is he who KEEPS THE WORDS of the prophecy in this book" (Revelation 22:7).

The Blessed Hope is *available* to ALL in the Church. Once the SPIRITUAL EARTHQUAKE takes place, however, the remaining Church will have missed out because of their own disobedience to the Word of God.

The Church is not appointed to go into the Tribulation. The Blessed Hope is still available to all believers.

QUESTION:

O. II Corinthians 5:10 says we must ALL appear before the Judgement Seat of Christ. How could this be if some are Raptured at the beginning, some at the end of the Tribulation period, and some at the end of the Millennium?

ANSWER:

Let's see what II Corinthians 5:9-10 says:

"So we make it our goal to please him, whether we are at home in the body or away from it. For we must all appear before the judgement seat of Christ, that each one may receive what is due him for the things done while in the body, whether good or bad."

The purpose of this judgement, is to give out rewards for faithful service. It will be based upon the good works of faithful servants.

The timing of this judgement is found in Revelation 11:18:

" . . . The time has come for judging the dead, and for rewarding your servants the prophets and your saints and those who reverence your name. . . . "

This judgement for rewards is right after the seventh trumpet, which places it at the end of the Tribulation and just prior to the Millennium.

The First Fruit believers and the Martyred Saints will be the only ones present at this portion of the judgement, since the rest of the Saints are not resurrected until the end of the Millennium. The remaining born-again believers, who missed the Kingdom, will not participate for two reasons:

(1) They don't have any rewards to receive.

(2) They missed the First Resurrection.

This is confirmed by Paul's teaching in I Corinthians 3:14:

" . . . his work will be shown for what it is, because the Day will bring it to light. It will be revealed with FIRE, and the FIRE will test the quality of each man's work. If what he has built survives, he will receive his reward. If it is burned up, he will suffer loss; he himself will be saved, but only as one ESCAPING THROUGH THE FLAMES."

The born-again believers who missed the Kingdom reign are saved, but they lose all of their rewards. They are pictured by Paul, as just escaping through the flames.

This is also seen in Revelation 20:12-15:

" . . . The dead were judged according to what they had done as recorded in the books . . . each person was judged according to what he had done. Then death and Hades were thrown into the lake of fire. The lake of fire is the second death. If anyone's name was not found written in the book of life, he was thrown into the lake of fire."

These born-again believers escape the flames of Hell because their names were written in the book of life. They pass their judgement seat, but miss out on any rewards.

QUESTION:

P. Revelation 13:18, says that the number of the beast or the Anti-christ is 666. Are there any indications who this man of sin actually is and proof his name adds up to 666?

ANSWER:

Revelation 13:18 reads:

"Here is wisdom. Let him that hath understanding count the number of the beast: for it is the number of a man; and his number is Six hundred threescore and six."

First of all, let's remember First Fruit Believers should be looking for the Blessed Hope (Titus 2:13) and not for the appearance of the Anti-christ.

However, notice the above Scripture implies the reader can determine who the Anti-christ is if wisdom is used. Wisdom is essentially God given understanding. It is intelligent, sensible, judicious and full of sound reasoning.

Before we go any further into this subject, we should get a firm footing of the things we know of this man of sin. We know he will come into his 42 month reign of terror, sometime during the Tribulation period. He will be the leader of the world and he will be hailed and worshiped as the messiah.

The world will marvel and wonder after this man. It will appear as if this man has come back from the dead — his fatal wound to the head miraculously healed as described in Revelation 13:3:

> "One of the heads of the beast seemed to have had a fatal wound, but the fatal wound had been healed. The whole world was astonished and followed the beast."

Notice it says he seemed to have a fatal wound. It suggests the wound was not a fatal wound as it appeared to be. This says there was a certain degree of deception surrounding his supposed death (Revelation 13:14).

Lyn Mize has written a fascinating booklet entitled: "MEAT IN DUE SEASON." (To order a copy, please see the order form in the back of this book.) This book reveals the most astounding fact: John F. Kennedy is the most likely candidate for the Antichrist.

The initial reaction to such a statement is one of complete unbelief. John Kennedy is dead. He couldn't be the Anti-christ. The whole world knows he died. Or, did he?

If he is the Anti-christ, then the numerical value of his name MUST = 666. The above Scripture says, "Let him that hath understanding count the number of the beast. . . ."

While attempting to count the number of his name, the Holy Spirit brought to mind: "Therefore shall a man leave his father and his mother, and shall cleave unto his wife: and THEY SHALL BE ONE FLESH" (Genesis 2:24).

In other words, in God's eyes, the husband and wife are ONE FLESH. In order to count the number of the man in Revelation 13:18 we need to add the names of both John and Jacqueline Kennedy to find his number. Quite REMARKABLY, as outlined on the next page, when we "count the number" of the letters in the name of the beast, they total exactly 666! You decide!

NUMBER OF
HIS NAME: 666
NAME: JOHN-JACQUELINE-KENNEDY

BASE: 3

NAME:		A 3	C 9	D 12	E 15	H 24	I 27	J 30	K 33	L 36	N 42	O 45	Q 51	U 63	Y 75
J	30	0	0	0	0	0	0	30	0	0	0	0	0	0	0
O	45	0	0	0	0	0	0	0	0	0	0	45	0	0	0
H	24	0	0	0	0	24	0	0	0	0	0	0	0	0	0
N	42	0	0	0	0	0	0	0	0	0	42	0	0	0	0
J	30	0	0	0	0	0	0	30	0	0	0	0	0	0	0
A	3	3	0	0	0	0	0	0	0	0	0	0	0	0	0
C	9	0	9	0	0	0	0	0	0	0	0	0	0	0	0
Q	51	0	0	0	0	0	0	0	0	0	0	0	51	0	0
U	63	0	0	0	0	0	0	0	0	0	0	0	0	63	0
E	15	0	0	0	15	0	0	0	0	0	0	0	0	0	0
L	36	0	0	0	0	0	0	0	0	36	0	0	0	0	0
I	27	0	0	0	0	0	27	0	0	0	0	0	0	0	0
N	42	0	0	0	0	0	0	0	0	0	42	0	0	0	0
E	15	0	0	0	15	0	0	0	0	0	0	0	0	0	0
K	33	0	0	0	0	0	0	0	33	0	0	0	0	0	0
E	15	0	0	0	15	0	0	0	0	0	0	0	0	0	0
N	42	0	0	0	0	0	0	0	0	0	42	0	0	0	0
N	42	0	0	0	0	0	0	0	0	0	42	0	0	0	0
E	15	0	0	0	15	0	0	0	0	0	0	0	0	0	0
D	12	0	0	12	0	0	0	0	0	0	0	0	0	0	0
Y	75	0	0	0	0	0	0	0	0	0	0	0	0	0	75
	666	3	9	12	60	24	27	60	33	36	168	45	51	63	75

(A base of 3 is used because Satan loves to mimic God. Three is the number of divine completion represented by the trinity of the Godhead: Father, Son and Holy Spirit. Satan copies with his unholy trinity: Satan, Anti-christ and the False Prophet.)

QUESTION:

Q. How was the length of the 42 generations from Abraham to Christ determined to be 2,166 years?

ANSWER:

The length of the 42 generations from Abraham to Christ was taken directly from the Word of God:

(A)   Abraham was 100 years old when his son Isaac was born (Genesis 21:5).

(B)   Isaac was 60 years old when his son Jacob was born (Genesis 25:26).

(C)   The Israelites lived in Egypt for 430 years (Exodus 12:40).

(D)   Jacob went to Egypt when he was 130 years old (Genesis 47:9).

(E)   King Solomon began construction of the Temple 480 years after the Israelites came out of Egypt (I Kings 6:1).

Adding the above together:

$$100 + 60 + 430 + 130 + 480 = 1,200$$

This tells us there were 1,200 years from Abraham until the construction of Solomon's Temple. Since the Temple was begun in the year 966 B.C., we only need to add 966 to 1,200, to determine that there were 2,166 years from Abraham until Christ.

The above lengths of time were recorded in the Word of God. One of the reasons may have been for a calculation such as this.

QUESTION:

R. What does it mean to be an overcomer?

ANSWER:

An overcomer is a believer who has had an authentic experience with God. Though thrown into the furnace of affliction, they have come forth as pure gold. The overcomer is born through the victory they receive by trusting in Jesus Christ.

Learning to be an overcomer is perhaps the most difficult thing to do on this earth as a human being. Possessing impressive credentials and degrees offer little solace when it comes to where the "rubber meets the road." Every professing Christian must <u>learn</u> to be an overcomer through faith and total trust in their Savior.

In Matthew 11:28-30, KJ Jesus urges:

> "Come unto me, all ye that labour and are heavy laden, and I will give you rest. Take my yoke upon you, and learn of me; for I am meek and lowly in heart: and ye shall find rest unto your souls. For my yoke is easy, and my burden is light."

The overcomers take their agony and burdens to the mighty counselor. Through prayer and trust, Jesus leads the downcast believer to "green pasture." The sting of the adversary is somehow turned to sweet victory. Christ alone is able to provide the peace that passes all understanding.

While every believer will have trials and testing in this world, Christ reminded us to be of good cheer because He <u>overcame this world</u>. As believers, we find our sweet victory in Him! He has already overcome for us. Overcomers are believers who find their strength and help in Him — not through man, but by the power of the Son of God.

A genuine overcomer follows in Christ's footsteps. They

learn to "take it on the chin" and to "take it to the cross." Whatever the world dishes out is handled with prayer and placed on the altar before God. By offering everything to Christ, they find hope and sufficiency in Him.

Being an overcomer is what being a Christian is all about. Through the trials of this life, the overcomer's faith is put on trial and thereby confirmed as Holy evidence before a mighty God, it is authentic.

As our example, Jesus endured the cross for the joy set before Him. Overcomers have the victory because of His victory. Through His victory, the overcomer is able to walk in newness of life. The overcomer knows: *they have been crucified with Christ*, their old life is gone (Galatians 2:20). By dying to self, the overcomer experiences the joy of Christ's triumph in their life.

Finally, an overcomer is grateful and humble: for they know of God's rich mercy and marvelous grace. If it wasn't for Christ, they would be doomed. Out of this gratitude, rises the song of gladness and praise. An overcomer's heart bursts forth with praise and adoration unto their God for the victory He provides.

The overcomer knows, firsthand, that while weeping may endure for the night: joy cometh in the morning!

QUESTION:

S.   Please discuss the difference between God's sacred calendar and the civil calendar.

ANSWER:

The civil calendar is believed to be the original calendar up until when God divinely instituted the sacred calendar:

> "The Lord said to Moses and Aaron in Egypt, "This month [Nisan] is to be for you the first month, the first month of your year" (Exodus 12:1).

The differences between the two calendars can be shown as follows:

NAMES OF MONTHS	MONTHS	GOD'S SACRED	JEWISH CIVIL
NISAN	March	1	7
IYAR	April	2	8
SIVAN	May	3	9
TAMMUZ	June	4	10
AV	July	5	11
ELUL	August	6	12
TISHRE	September	7	1
CHESHVAN	October	8	2
KISLEV	November	9	3
TEVET	December	10	4
SHEVAT	January	11	5
ADAR I	February	12	6
ADAR II		LEAP YR.	LEAP YR.

Examples: The second month on the civil calendar falls in Cheshvan or October. The ninth month on God's sacred calendar falls in Kislev or November-December. (Note: the Jewish months overlap our regular months.)

QUESTION:

T. What did Jesus mean by: "Occupy until I come?"

ANSWER:

This verse is found in Luke 19:13, which is the parable of the ten pounds. Jesus was teaching us that His faithful followers should be diligent until He returns.

In the past, when people thought the Lord was about to return, they quit their jobs and sold their possessions. Unless the Lord told the individual to do this, this type of behavior is contrary to what the previous verse teaches.

The believer should be diligently doing whatever they have been called to do. At the same time, however, some take the above verse as an excuse for not looking for Him.

This extreme is not correct either. The believer should be diligent; but, at the same time, should also be LOOKING for the Lord to return.

Looking for Him is an attitude of the person's heart. While we should continue living our lives doing what the Lord has called us to do, we should also understand that this world is NOT our home. The believer's true home is in Heaven, and we are really strangers just passing through this world. (See I Peter 2:11 & I John 2:15.)

The believer needs to learn to balance diligently working at those things they have been called to do, along with LOOKING for and eagerly awaiting His soon return.

QUESTION:

U. What is the difference between those described in the 5th seal (Revelation 6:9-11) and the Great Multitude of Revelation 7:9-17?

ANSWER:

We can't be certain, but note the following:

Those described in the 5th seal are said to be given robes, while those described as the Great Multitude in Revelation 7 are said to be washing their robes.

The first group did not appear to previously have any robes, while the second group did. This may mean the first group represents individuals who were not saved prior to when the Tribulation period began. They received Jesus as their Savior after the Tribulation began, and were GIVEN white robes.

The second group has been discussed in this book as the Great

Multitude of born-again believers who had to enter the Tribulation because they had soiled their garments prior to when it began. They are pictured in Revelation 7, as washing their robes and making them white again in the blood of the Lamb.

QUESTION:

V. What about the Feast of Trumpets, could the Rapture take place on this Feast?

ANSWER:

Popular Tradition has convinced most people that the Feast of Trumpets is the only day the Rapture can take place. As we have seen in this book, there are other dates which are more likely.

Students of Bible Prophecy know that the first four Feasts have seen either their fulfillment or partial fulfillment:

Passover	Jesus died
Unleavened Bread	Jesus was buried
Firstfruits	Jesus rose
Pentecost	Church was born

This book has shown that Pentecost is a very likely time for the Rapture. If the birth of the Church is only a partial fulfillment of that Feast, then the Rapture should also occur on that day to fulfill it completely.

However, if Pentecost was completely fulfilled with the birth of the Church, then it is possible for the Rapture to occur on the Feast of Trumpets.

The Feast of Trumpets is the next Feast in line after Pentecost. And since God has fulfilled the Feasts in the order given, the Rapture could occur on this Feast.

QUESTION:

W. Please discuss the Judgement Seat of Christ.

ANSWER:

The Judgement Seat of Christ is described in II Corinthians 5:9-10:

> "So we make it our goal to please him, whether we are at home in the body or away from it. For we must all appear before the judgement seat of Christ, that each one may receive what is due him for the things done while in the body, whether good or bad."

The purpose of this judgement, is to give out rewards for faithful service. It will be a time for the Lord to review every individual's life for both good and bad. For all the good things that were done, the believer will receive rewards. The Word of God indicates that there are five possible crowns that can be obtained:

VICTOR'S CROWN

> "Everyone who competes in the games goes into strict training. They do it to get a crown that will not last; but we do it to get a CROWN that will LAST FOR-EVER.
>
> "Therefore I do not run like a man running aimlessly; I do not fight like a man beating the air. No, I beat my body and make it my slave so that after I have preached to others, I myself will not be disqualified for the prize" (I Corinthians 9:25-27).

MARTYR'S CROWN

> "Do not be afraid of what you are about to suffer. I tell you, the devil will put some of you in prison to test

you, and you will suffer persecution for ten days. Be faithful, even to the point of death, and I will give you the CROWN OF LIFE" (Revelation 2:10).

ELDER'S CROWN

"Be shepherds of God's flock that is under your care, serving as overseers - not because you must, but because you are willing, as God wants you to be; not greedy for money, but eager to serve; not lording it over those entrusted to you, but being examples to the flock. And when the Chief Shepherd appears, you will receive the CROWN OF GLORY that will never fade away (I Peter 5:2-4).

SOUL WINNER'S CROWN

"For what is our hope, or joy, or CROWN OF REJOICING? Are not even ye in the presence of our Lord Jesus Christ at his coming? For ye are our glory and joy" (I Thessalonians 2:19-20, KJ).

CROWN OF RIGHTEOUSNESS

"Henceforth there is laid up for me a CROWN OF RIGHTEOUSNESS, which the Lord, the righteous judge, shall give me at that day: and not to me only, but unto all them also that love his appearing" (II Timothy 4:8, KJ).

For all believers who have faithfully served the Lord, the Judgement Seat of Christ will be a glorious day indeed. The crowns outlined above will never fade away. Also remember, Jesus warned us ahead of time: don't let anyone take your crown! (Revelation 3:11).

QUESTION:

X. Why is the Blessed Hope important to the believer?

ANSWER:

The Blessed Hope is so very important to the believer for several reasons.

First of all, looking for the Blessed Hope of the Lord's soon return is sound doctrine. The reader is encouraged to read the first and second chapters of Titus where Paul tells the importance of sound doctrine.

Sound doctrine should be encouraged and taught. Any who refute sound doctrine should be rebuked and encouraged back to sound doctrine.

"Looking for that Blessed Hope . . . " is sound doctrine that needs to be taught to all believers.

Second of all, having the Blessed Hope, the believers will purify themselves:

"Everyone who has this hope in him purifies himself, just as he is pure" (I John 3:3).

Knowing that the Lord will return very soon, the believers know that they will stand before a Holy God at that time. Having this hope in their heart, the believers are motivated to live a holy and blameless life. They will want to purify their hearts, knowing they will be with Him very soon.

Finally, as was noted in the last question, one of the crowns that can be obtained is the CROWN OF RIGHTEOUSNESS, for those who LOVE HIS APPEARING.

Those who LOVE HIS APPEARING will be given a crown. Having the Blessed Hope in one's heart should motivate the believer to long for and truly love the thought of being with Him.

This will result in the believer receiving a glorious crown.

The Blessed Hope is a very important hope that every believer should have.

QUESTION:

Y. What is the order of major events during the Tribulation?

ANSWER:

The following is a highlight of the major events that are about to transpire on this planet. These are listed in their order chronologically:

1) Rapture of First Fruit believers.

2) Anti-christ is revealed and a strong delusion is sent out by God.

3) Two witnesses arrive and Angel proclaims eternal gospel.

4) 144,000 Jews sealed.

5) Peace covenant signed.

6) World War III (Gog-Magog War).

7) Famine & Death over one-fourth of the earth.

8) Christians Martyred for Jesus.

9) Temple worship restored in Israel.

10) Satan is cast to the earth to indwell the body of the Anti-christ for a 42 month reign of power.

11) Anti-christ ends sacrifices and creates abomination of desolation.

12) The Jewish remnant flees to safety.

13) The two Jewish witnesses are killed and then resurrected three days later.

14) God pours out His wrath.

15) Earth is harvested.

16) Jesus Christ returns with His Saints for the Battle of Armageddon.

17) Anti-christ and False Prophet thrown into the lake of fire for 1,000 years.

18) Judgement Seat of Christ.

19) Millennium reign for 1,000 years.

20) Satan let loose for a short time for one final battle on earth, after which he is cast into hell forever.

21) Great White Throne Judgement: with all whose names are not found written in the Book of Life, being thrown into the lake of fire.

(Note: Some events happen near the same time, so the above chronology may require slight adjustment.)

QUESTION:

Z. Haven't you forgotten that we are saved by Grace?

ANSWER:

God's Grace is provided for believers to be overcomers. His Grace is not divine favor extended to the believer for continuance in any form of unholy behavior.

His Grace enables committed believers, empowered by His Spirit, through genuine repentance, to be overcomers. By God's Grace, through faith in Christ, the believer is able to break the chains of darkness and live a victorious life in Him.

Christ, alone, is able to heal and make whole. His beautiful gift of Grace is sufficient. Being justified by His Grace, we have the hope of eternal life:

"... having been justified by His grace, we might become heirs having the hope of eternal life. This is a trustworthy saying. And I want you to stress these things, so that those who have trusted in God may be careful to devote themselves to doing what is good" (Titus 3:7 & 8).

This position of Grace is sacred, and should be deeply respected.

Too many people have misunderstood God's Grace. Often His Grace is perceived as a level of assurance which enables them to go along in their same uncommitted behavior. Erroneously, they believe God's Grace will counteract their uncommitted and unyielded life. They have assumed Grace means *erase*, with no consequences for their actions.

While we are saved by Grace, our salvation does not assure us that we will be found worthy to escape the Tribulation period. While salvation is completely free, escape from the Tribulation and entrance into the Kingdom will be based upon how the believer has utilized that free gift.

Peter tells us in II Peter 3:18: "... **GROW** in the **grace** and knowledge of our Lord and Savior Jesus Christ...." Peter is reminding the believer to continue to grow in God's grace. To grow in His grace means to make every effort to be found spotless, blameless and at peace with Him (see II Peter 3:10-18). Through the sanctifying work of the Spirit, the believer will grow in the Grace of God.

The overcoming First Fruit believer realizes that he has to *give over* **all** areas of his life to be triumphant **by** His marvelous Grace. This is completely different from the "lukewarm" view which says that God's Grace will ***look over*** those areas because of His Grace. Grace then becomes a bandage to cover an unclean life. As Jude 4, says:

"For certain men whose condemnation was written about long ago have secretly slipped in among you. They are godless men, who change the GRACE of God into a license for immorality."

We are justified freely by God's marvelous Grace (Romans 3:24). That Grace, however, should not be used as a license to sin. God will not be mocked.

Jesus is our answer, not our excuse.

SUMMARY OF KEY DATES

	FEAST OF PENTECOST (A)	FEAST OF TRUMPETS	17th DAY OF SECOND MONTH (B)	24th day of NINTH MONTH
1993	5/26-5/30	9/16-17	11/01	12/08
1994	5/16-5/22	9/06-07	10/22	11/27
1995	6/04-6/04	9/25-26	11/10	12/17
1996	5/24-5/26	9/14-15	10/30	12/05
1997	6/11-6/15	10/02-03	11/17	12/23
1998	5/31-5/31	9/21-22	11/06	12/13
1999	5/21-5/23	9/11-12	10/27	12/03
2000	6/09-6/11	9/30-10/1	11/15	12/22

(A) The first date given for Pentecost represents the sixth day of Sivan. The second date represents 50 days after the feast of first fruits (see Leviticus 23).

(B) As mentioned in Chapter 10, another interpretation for the 17th day of the second month is to calculate it based upon the Fall equinox. In the year of the Flood, the 17th day of the second month would have been 47 days (30+17) after the Fall equinox which was on September 21. Therefore, the date of the Flood is believed to be November 7. It is possible for the Rapture to take place on the anniversary of the Flood.

The Day of the Lord

Hidden within God's description of the Day of the Lord is an amazing chronology of end-time events about to take place on this planet.

Obadiah 15, says, "The Day of the Lord is near for ALL NATIONS." The recent war in the Gulf is evidence the Day of the Lord is about to begin, and it will involve ALL NATIONS.

Amos 5:18 describes it: "Woe to you who long for the Day of the Lord! Why do you long for the Day of the Lord? That day will be DARKNESS not light. It will be as though a man fled from a lion only to meet a bear, as though he entered his house and rested his hand on the wall only to have a snake bite him." This time will be the most terrible time for the inhabitants of the earth. Some of the various titles God uses to describe this time include:

	Reference
A Cruel Day, with Wrath and Fierce Anger	Isaiah 13:19
Day of His Burning Anger	Isaiah 13:13
Day of Vengeance	Isaiah 34:8
Day of Slaughter	Jeremiah 12:3
Day of Disaster	Jeremiah 17:17
Time of Jacob's Trouble	Jeremiah 30:7
Day of the Lord's Wrath	Ezekiel 7:19
Day of Clouds	Ezekiel 30:3
Day of Darkness and Gloom	Joel 2:2

The above are just a sample of some of the names God uses to describe the time He has appointed to judge the nations. The pages that follow compare Jeremiah, Ezekiel, and Joel. These three Prophets all discuss the same subjects and reveal the chronology of events that are about to take place on the earth.

DAY OF THE LORD

JEREMIAH	*EZEKIEL*	*JOEL*
RESTORE LAND	**RESTORE LAND**	**RESTORE LAND**
"... I WILL ... RESTORE them to the land I gave their forefathers to possess ..." (CH. 30:3).	"... I will resettle your towns, and the ruins will be rebuilt. The desolate land will be cultivated instead of lying desolate in the sight of all who pass through it. They will say, 'This land that was laid waste had become like the GARDEN OF EDEN ...'" (CH. 36:34-35).	"Before them the land is like the GARDEN OF EDEN ..." (CH. 2:3).
RETURN OF PEOPLE	**RETURN OF PEOPLE**	**RETURN OF PEOPLE**
"... I will bring MY PEOPLE Israel and Judah back from captivity and restore them to the land I gave their forefathers to possess ..." (CH. 30:3).	"I will take the Israelites out of the nations where they have gone. I will gather them from all around and bring them back to into their land" (CH. 37:21).	"Before them the land is like the GARDEN OF EDEN ..." (CH. 2:3).
TEMPLE RESTORED	**TEMPLE RESTORED**	**TEMPE RESTORED**
"I will restore the fortunes of Jacob's tents and have compassion on his dwellings; the city will be rebuilt on her ruins, and the PALACE [TEMPLE] will stand in its proper place" (CH. 30:18).	"... I will establish them and increase their numbers, and I will put my SANCTUARY among them. . . . Then the nations will know that I the Lord make Israel holy, when my SANCTUARY is among them . . ." (CH. 37:26-27).	"Blow the trumpet in Zion, declare a holy fast, call a sacred assembly. Gather the people, consecrate the assembly. . . . Let the priests, who minister before the Lord, weep between the TEMPLE porch and the altar" (CH. 2:15-17).

Restore Land

Jeremiah, Ezekiel and Joel all record similar descriptions of the time when Israel will see their land restored. Notice they record the fact it is God Himself who will restore them.

People who visit Israel say it looks like the Garden of Eden compared to its former state. This portion of Scripture has been fulfilled!

Return of People

After God restored the land of Israel in Ezekiel 36, God brings the people back to the land in Ezekiel 37. This prophecy never was possible until May 14, 1948, when Israel was re-established as a nation. Since the nation of Israel has been re-established, God's chosen people have been returning to their land from all around the world.

This return to the land will continue, and will turn into the *SECOND EXODUS* immediately after the outbreak of the Gog-Magog war that is described in the next section.

Temple Restored

One of the next prophecies to take place in Israel should be the restoration of the site for the Temple. Jewish religious leaders have been busy making the various utensils to be used once the Temple has been erected. Many Bible students believe the Temple will be erected adjacent to the Dome of the Rock, and that it will be accomplished relatively quickly since it can be constructed as a tent.

Once Israel restores the Temple, watch out! The very next prophecy recorded in Ezekiel 38, is the Gog-Magog war. This could be the final thing to provoke the Arab nations into a holy war. They will align with Russia against the land of Israel to begin the Day of the Lord.

DAY OF THE LORD

JEREMIAH
GOG-MAGOG WAR

"See, the STORM of the Lord will burst out in WRATH, a driving wind swirling down on the heads of the wicked. The FIERCE ANGER of the LORD will not turn back until he fully accomplishes the purpose of his heart. IN DAYS TO COME YOU WILL UNDERSTAND THIS" (CH. 30:23-24).

"Though I completely destroy all the nations among which I scatter you, I will not completely destroy you" (CH. 30:11).

EZEKIEL
GOG-MAGOG WAR

"You will come from your place in the far NORTH. . . . You will advance against my people Israel like a CLOUD. . . . I will bring you against my land, so that the nations may know me when I show myself holy through you before their eyes" (CH.38:14-16).

"I will turn you [Russia] around, put hooks in your jaws and bring you out with your whole army, and a great horde . . . your HORSES, your HORSEMEN fully armed and a great horde. . . . I will summon a sword against Gog [Russia] on all my mountains declares the Sovereign Lord. Every man's sword will be against his brother. I will execute judgement upon him with plague and bloodshed; I will pour down TORRENTS of rain, hailstones and BURNING SULFUR on him and on his troops and on the many nations with him" (CH 38:4, 21, 22).

JOEL
GOG-MAGOG WAR

" . . . the Day of the Lord is coming. It is close at hand — a day of DARKNESS AND GLOOM. Like dawn spreading across the mountains a large and mighty army comes. . . . I will drive the NORTH-ERN army far from you" (CH.2:1, 2, 20).

"Before them FIRE devours, behind them a flame blazes. Before them the land is like the garden of Eden, behind them a desert WASTE — NOTHING ESCAPES THEM. They have the appearance of HORSES; they gallop along like CALVARY. With a noise like that of chariots they leap over the mountains" (CH. 2:3-5).

"I will drive the NORTHERN ARMY [Russia] far from you, pushing it into a parched and barren land. . . . And its stench will go up its smell will rise" (CH 2:20).

Gog-Magog War

The Gog-Magog war will be one of the most surprising wars in the history of mankind. I Thessalonians 5:2-3 warns, " . . . the Day of the Lord will come like a thief in the night. While people are saying, 'PEACE and SAFETY,' DESTRUCTION will come on THEM SUDDENLY, as labor pains on a pregnant woman, and they will not escape."

Just prior to the outbreak of the war, people of the world will be thinking there will be peace in the world. The leaders of the world have declared an end to the cold war. We are nearing the point when nations of the earth will all believe the time of peace and safety has finally arrived. When that point arrives, the Gog-Magog war will erupt to begin God's Judgement.

Nations

The following Scripture verses indicate the nations that will be aligned during this terrible war that begins the Day of the Lord's Wrath and Anger:

Ezekiel 30:3-5

"For the day is near, the day of the Lord is near — a day of CLOUDS, a time of doom for the NATIONS. A sword will come against EGYPT, and anguish will come upon CUSH.

"When the slain fall in Egypt, her wealth will be carried away and her foundations torn down. CUSH and PUT, LYDIA and all of Arabia, LIBYA and the people of the covenant land [ie, in countries in league with Egypt] will fall by the sword along with EGYPT."

These events outlined in Ezekiel 30, are the same as those outlined in Ezekiel 38 and 39, as well as those described in Daniel 11:40-43.

Ezekiel 38:4, 5 & 9

"I will turn you [Russia] around, put hooks in your jaws and bring you out with your whole army — your HORSES, your HORSEMEN fully armed, and a great horde with large and small shields all of them brandishing their swords. Persia, CUSH and PUT will be with them. . . . You and all your troops and many NATIONS with you will go up, advancing like a storm; you will be like a CLOUD covering the land."

Ezekiel 38:21 & 22

"I will summon a sword against Gog on all my mountains, declares the Sovereign Lord. Every man's sword will be against his brother. I will execute judgement upon him with plague and bloodshed; I will pour down torrents of rain, hailstones and burning sulfur on him and on his troops and on the many NATIONS with him."

Daniel 11:40-43

"At the time of the end the king of the South (Egypt) will engage him (Anti-christ) in battle, and the king of the North (Russia) will storm out against him with chariots & cavalry and a great fleet of ships. He (Anti-christ) will invade many countries and sweep through them like a flood. He will also invade the beautiful land (Israel). Many countries will fall, but Edom, Moab and the leaders of Ammon will be delivered from his hand. He will extend his power over many countries; EGYPT will not escape. He will gain control of the treasures of gold and silver and all the riches of EGYPT, with the LYBYANS and Nubians in submission."

As can be seen from the above references, Russia will align itself with many nations. The modern day names for these various nations are shown below:

Cush	=	Ethiopia
Put	=	Lybia
Persia	=	Iran
Edom, Moab	=	Jordan

Seven Year Period

The above reference in Daniel 11:40, brings another party into this war. It says that the King of the South (Egypt) and the King of the North (Russia) come against "him." This person is the Anti-christ. Daniel 9:27, tells us how he will begin and end:

"He will confirm a covenant with many for one 'seven' [7 Years] but in the middle of that 'seven' he will put an end to SACRIFICE and OFFERING. And one who causes desolation will place abomination on a wing of the TEMPLE until the end that is decreed is poured out on him."

Now we can see that the Anti-christ will come on the scene at the beginning of the seven year Tribulation period and confirm a covenant with many. Notice it also indicates Temple sacrifice will be restored, which the Anti-christ will later put an end to.

There are some who believe that the Gog-Magog war will begin in the middle of this Tribulation period. This would be impossible for three reasons:

First, Ezekiel indicates that the Temple is restored and then the war breaks out. This is confirmed by Daniel who reveals the Temple is restored up until the middle of the seven year period. After that time there is no longer any worshiping at the Temple. To place the Gog-Magog war in the middle of the Tribulation would be out of line with Ezekiel, Daniel, Jeremiah, and Joel.

Second, Ezekiel 39:9 indicates there will be a seven year

period of time that Israel will burn the weapons of this terrible war:

"Then those who live in the towns of Israel will go out and use the weapons for fuel and burn them up — the small and large shields, the bows and arrows, the war clubs and spears. FOR SEVEN YEARS they will use them for fuel."

If the Gog-Magog war began in the middle of the Tribulation, they would still be burning the weapons at the beginning of the 1,000 year millennium.This is supposed to be the start of the reign with Christ, not a very appropriate time to be burning the weapons of war.

Finally, as can be seen on the next page that is entitled the "SECOND EXODUS," the Jewish people will be coming back to the land of Israel in a fashion similar to their first Exodus out of Egypt. It is quite clear that this mass exodus is immediately after the great Gog-Magog war. It would be impossible for the SECOND EXODUS to occur at the middle of the Tribulation period because that is the time when the Anti-christ will close down the Temple and chase the Jewish people out of Israel. This is described in Revelation 12:6:

"The woman [Israel] fled into the desert to a place prepared for her by God, where she might be taken care of for 1,260 days."

If the Gog-Magog war were in the middle, the Jews would return to Israel at the same time the Anti-christ begins to pursue her! This is not possible. It is quite clear, the Gog-Magog war can not occur at the mid point, but must begin near the very start of the Tribulation period; to begin the terrible Day of the Lord.

DAY OF THE LORD

JEREMIAH SECOND EXODUS

"See, I will bring them from the land of the NORTH [Russia] and gather them from the ends of the earth. AMONG THEM will be the BLIND and LAME, EXPECTANT MOTHERS and WOMEN IN LABOR; a GREAT THRONG will return. They will come with WEEPING; they will pray as I bring them back... For the Lord will ransom JACOB and redeem them from the hand of those stronger then they" (CH 31:8, 9, 11).

"You brought your people Israel out of Egypt with signs and wonders, by a mighty hand and an outstanding arm and with great terror. I will surely gather them from ALL the lands where I banish them, in MY FURIOUS ANGER and GREAT WRATH; I will bring them back to their place and let them live in safety" (CH. 32:21,37).

NOTE: *Jeremiah indicated that their second EXODUS will include women in labor. This would indicate a sudden return from Russia. Also notice that they return to live in safety.*

EZEKIEL SECOND EXODUS

"I will NOW bring JACOB back from captivity.... I will gather them to their own land not leaving ANY behind" (CH. 39:25,28).

NOTE: *This occurs immediately AFTER the God-Magog war. Immediately after the SECOND EXODUS there is great prosperity and God pours out His Spirit on the house of Israel. (See Next Section)*

JOEL SECOND EXODUS

"Even now, declares the Lord, return to me with all your heart, with fasting and weeping and mourning.... Let them say, SPARE YOUR PEOPLE, O LORD..." (CH 2:12, 17).

NOTE:

September 29, 1990, Jerusalem Post: Russian Aliya (immigration) FAR EXCEEDS EXPECTATIONS. Over a million Russian Jews will make aliya by the end of 1992, and another million by 1995 — far surpassing previous estimates, Jewish Agency Chairman Simcha Dinitz told a Jerusalem press conference last week.

Since there are only an estimated 2 million Jews in Russia, the SECOND EXODUS must occur very soon. At current rates, they would all be out of Russia by 1995. Jeremiah 31:8 clearly shows a GREAT THRONG coming our of Russia. This has to happen very soon!

DAY OF THE LORD

JEREMIAH **PROSPERITY**	*EZEKIEL* **PROSPERITY**	*JOEL* **PROSPERITY**
"They will come and shout for joy on the heights of Zion; they will rejoice in the BOUNTY of the Lord — the GRAIN, the NEW WINE, and the OIL . . . ." (CH. 31:12).	"But now the Lord God says, I will end the captivity of my people and have mercy upon them and RESTORE THEIR FORTUNES" (CH. 39:25, LB).	"He sends you abundant showers, both autumn and spring rains, as before, the Threshing floors will be FILLED with GRAIN; the vats will overflow with NEW WINE and OIL" (CH. 2:23, 24).
GOD'S SPIRIT	**GOD'S SPIRIT**	**GOD'S SPIRIT**
	"I will no longer hide my face from them for I will POUR OUT MY SPIRIT on the house of Israel, declares the Sovereign Lord" (CH. 39:29).	"And afterward, I will POUR OUR MY SPIRIT on all people. Your sons and daughters will prophecy, your old men will dream dreams, your young men will see visions. Even on my servants, both men and women, I will POUR OUT MY SPIRIT in those days" (CH 2:28, 29).
		NOTE: *It is clear that Joel says that this will happen in the period known as the day of the Lord.*

It can be seen from the above, that God has certain plans for His people during the start of the period known as the Day of the Lord. God will bring them back from ALL over the earth including a mass SECOND EXODUS out of Russia. This occurs immediately after the Gog-Magog war in which God defeats Russia.

After God brings Israel back, He restores them and abundantly blesses them. There will be no doubt about it. It is God who will do it all (see Jeremiah 33:9).

After the terrible Gog-Magog war, the very beginning of the Day of the Lord will be a great time of peace and prosperity for the people of Israel. For the rest of the world, however, it will be a terrible time of darkness, disaster and gloom. People will be forced to follow the Anti-christ, and the Christians who are not included in the Rapture of First Fruit Believers will be persecuted for their faith.

The Day of the Lord is near. Prepare your hearts to meet the Lord before that great Day arrives!

Glossary

ARMAGEDDON
That great battle at the end of the Tribulation period where Jesus Christ returns with His Saints to defeat the Anti-christ and his armies (Revelation 16:16).

BLESSED HOPE
The glorious promise that Jesus Christ will return for His own prior to the Tribulation (Titus 2:13).

BRIDE
Those born-again believers who have prepared themselves to meet the Lord (Revelation 19:7-9). (Also see First Fruit believer and Over-comer.)

BRIDEGROOM
Jesus Christ (Revelation 19:9, and Matthew 25:5).

DAY OF LORD
Period of time that begins with the Tribulation period. Also includes the 1,000 year period known as the Millennium (I Thessalonians 5:2 & 4).

FIRST COMING
Christ's first arrival on the scene of human history. Best estimates of the time He was born are 3 B.C. to 1 B.C.

FIRST FRUIT
BELIEVER
Born-again believer found worthy by the Lord to be Raptured prior to the Tribulation period. Also referred to as an Overcomer or as the Bride of Christ.

Called the Male child in Revelation 12:5 (Revelation 14:4, Revelation 2:26-27 and Revelation 3:10).

HARVEST

Gathering of all who remain at the end of the Tribulation period (Revelation 14:14-20, Luke 3:17 and Matthew 13:30).

KINGDOM

The 1,000 year reign with Jesus Christ as the King of Kings. Also known as the Millennium (Revelation 20:5-6 & Luke 20:35).

MALE CHILD

The First Fruit believer or the Saint known as an Overcomer. Taken up to the Throne of God prior to the Tribulation since he was considered worthy to escape (Revelation 12:5; Revelation 14:4 and Revelation 2:26-27).

MARTYR

Those born-again believers who stand up for Jesus Christ and die for Him (Revelation 2:10; Revelation 7:9-17; Revelation 12:17, Revelation 14:12-13 and Revelation 20:4-6).

MILLENNIUM

The 1,000 year reign with Jesus Christ as King. Also known as the Kingdom, or the 7th day or the last 1,000 years of God's 7,000 years of man (Revelation 20:4).

NOMINAL CHRISTIAN

A person who calls himself a christian, but in reality is not truly born-again. Also known as a Professing Christian (II Timothy 3:5 and I John 1:4).

OVERCOMER

Born-again believer who has died to self and lives to please God by a holy, righteous and blameless walk. One who has kept the Word of God and is looking for the soon return of the Lord. Also see, First Fruit believer, Male child and the Bride. (See Chapter 5.)

PENTECOST

Feast that falls on the 6th day of Sivan. Known as the Feast of Weeks, the Feast of Harvest and the day of Firstfruits. The day that Enoch was born and Raptured. Church began at Pentecost, and it is very possible that the Rapture of the First Fruit believers will also take place on this Feast (Exodus 23:14-16; Exodus 34:22; and Numbers 28:26).

PROPHETIC YEAR

Length of year as measured by God: 360 days. See Chapter 8 and Genesis 7:11 and 8:3. (As opposed to a Solar year which is 365.25 days long.)

RAPTURE

Removal of born-again believers from the earth. Enoch being a type-picture for the First Fruit believers (Genesis 5:24). The Rapture of First Fruit believers is found in Revelation 12:5 and Revelation 14:1-5. Also referred to in II Thessalonians 2:7.

SECOND COMING

The return of the Lord at the end of the Tribulation period and at the end of the 6,000 years of man (Revelation 14:14-20, Revelation 20:11-21 & Matthew 24:30-31) Saints return with the Lord at this time as shown in Jude 14, to judge everyone and to rule with an iron scepter (Revelation 2:27).

TRIBULATION

Period of time that begins right after the Rapture of First Fruit believers. Should begin with the rider on the white horse (the Anti-christ) probably signing a peace covenant. Period lasts approximately 7 years, but could be slightly shorter. Ends with the return of the Lord at His Second Coming with His saints at the battle of Armageddon.

UPWARD CALLING   High calling referred to by the Apostle Paul in Philippians 3:14. For those Saints alive when the Tribulation is about to begin, it refers to escaping that time. It also is referring to being included in the First Resurrection and reigning with the Lord during the Kingdom or the Millennium.

WATCHING   An attitude of the heart that is truly looking for the soon return of the Lord. It was commanded by the Lord and it includes the following:

1) Being aware of prophetic signs in God's Word.
2) Living a life of Holiness.
3) Living a life separated from the world.
4) Encouraging one another with the wonderful Hope of His soon return.
5) Telling others Jesus is coming again very soon.
6) Praying Jesus will *count you worthy to escape* all that is about to happen.

Epilogue

As I finish this work, the Lord reminded me of His words spoken through the prophet Habakkuk:

"Write down the revelation and make it plain on tablets so that a herald [or: so that whoever reads it] may run with it" (Habakkuk 2:2).

It is my prayer that I have made the message clear to those who have "eyes to see" and "ears to hear." It is up to you now to heed this message and to tell others while there is still time.

The vast majority of people will not understand, but the wise will understand. The current Church of Laodicea needs to be reminded:

"If my people, who are called by my name, will humble themselves and pray and seek my face and turn from their wicked ways, then will I hear from heaven and will forgive their sin and will heal their land" (II Chronicles 7:14).

May God use this message to wake-up and prepare His people to meet Him.

About the Author

Jim Harman has been a Christian for over 15 years. He has diligently studied the Word of God, with particular emphasis on Prophecy. Jim's first book, *THE BLESSED HOPE*, was widely distributed around the world. It encouraged many to continue LOOKING for the Lord's soon return, and brought many to a saving knowledge of Jesus Christ.

Jim's professional experience includes being a Certified Public Accountant and a Certified Property Manager. He has a background in both public accounting and real estate management with several well known national firms.

Jim had previously believed all born-again believers were included in the Rapture. This new book: *THE COMING SPIRITUAL EARTHQUAKE* is the result of a great deal of prayer, study and research into the Word of God.

It is Jim's strong desire many will take this timely message to heart. He feels God has called him to write this book in the hope souls will be saved and a great multitude of Christians will be prepared to meet Jesus.

Jim has said, "If I am wrong, anyone who follows the directions given in this book will be better off spiritually. If I am right, they will be among the few to escape the greatest spiritual calamity of the ages."

SPECIAL OFFER

Jim and Cindy Harman co-author **PROPHECY COUNT-DOWN**, a newsletter to keep the Bride of Christ alert to signs of the time. The purpose of this prophecy newsletter is to help the Believer's heart maintain an inner watchfulness by kindling a fire of faith and hope in Christ and fanning it with facts, Biblical Truths, and world events until the coming of our Lord.

Order your one year subscription today, and receive a free copy of Lyn Mize's new book: *MEAT IN DUE SEASON*. This book includes a startling revelation of who the Anti-christ may be, as well as the nation most likely to be Babylon the Great. Must reading!

JIM HARMAN MINISTRIES

P.O. BOX 941612   MAITLAND, FL 32794
(407) 834-4106

The author of this book is available for speaking engagements. Please contact him at the above address or call him at: (407) 834-4106.

ORDER FORM

ITEMS:	PRICE	QTY	TOTAL
COMING SPIRITUAL EARTHQUAKE (3 for $25)	$10.00 ————		$ ————
SPIRITUAL EARTHQUAKE (AUDIO) (Book on 3 cassette tapes)	$10.00 ————		$ ————
THE BLESSED HOPE (3 for $10)	$ 5.00 ————		$ ————
BEYOND THE HIGHER POWER (God's solution to the drug problem)	$ 7.00 ————		$ ————
PROPHECY COUNTDOWN SPECIAL** (See page 173)	$20.00 ————		$ ————
MEAT IN DUE SEASON (LYN MIZE) (See Question P)	$ 5.00 ————		$ ————
SUB-TOTAL			$ ————
SALES TAX @ 7% (FLA Residents Only)			$ ————
TOTAL AMOUNT OF ORDER *(Postage & Handling Included.)*			$ ————

Send check or money order to:

JIM HARMAN MINISTRIES
P.O. BOX 941612, MAITLAND, FL 32794
(407) 834-4106

Name _____

Address _____

City, State, Zip _____

***Free copy of Lyn Mize's new book: **MEAT IN DUE SEASON** with all one year subscriptions to **PROPHECY COUNTDOWN**.*

The Day of the Lord is Near!

The Coming Spiritual Earthquake

by James T. Harman

"The Message presented in this book is greatly needed to awaken believers to the false ideas many have when it comes to the Rapture. I might have titled it: THE RAPTURE EARTH-QUAKE!"
Ray Brubaker - God's News Behind the News

"If I am wrong, anyone who follows the directions given in this book will be better off spiritually. If I am right, they will be among the few to escape the greatest spiritual calamity of the ages."
Jim Harman - Author

MUST READING FOR EVERY CHRISTIAN!
HURRY! BEFORE IT IS TOO LATE!